Chitterne

a Wiltshire Village

BY

SUE ROBINSON

First published in the United Kingdom in 2007 by The Hobnob Press,
PO Box 1838, East Knoyle, Salisbury SP3 6FA.

British Library Cataloguing in Publication Data
A catalogue record for this book is available from the British Library.

ISBN 978-0-946418-68-8

Typeset in 11/16 pt Scala
Typesetting and origination by John Chandler
Printed in Great Britain by Salisbury Printing Company Ltd, Salisbury

Picture Credits

My thanks to Christian Mould who drew the pictures of Chitterne Barn on pages 128 & 129, and the following people who kindly lent or copied photographs and postcards for use in this book. Other pictures and maps are by me. I apologise if I have missed anyone with an earlier claim to ownership.

Front cover: the old smithy. Back cover: Chitterne Church and the Green.

Dewey Museum, Warminster *vi*, 91, 92
Local Studies Library, Trowbridge 17, 18, 56, 57
Alan Sprack pages: 6, 12, 24, 25, 29, 51, 54, 78, 88, 93, 105, 112, 113, 135
Cheryl Nicol 14
Doug Young 15
Pete Ash book cover, 20, 38, 40, 47, 48, 52, 61, 76, 111, 145
Dave Bamford 28, 93, 122, 127
Ivy Maidment 27, 84
Diana Sanders 35

Bill Windsor 55, 64, 69, 80
Graham Dean 117
The late Bert Bailey 32, 136, 143
Ray Poolman 144
Richard Essberger 40
Jeanne George 67, 118
Sally Hudson 83
Fred Babey 87, 94, 95, 97, 139, 141, 142
Ray Feltham 140
Chris Gaskell map 3
Dave Robinson 2, 41, 42, 46, 109, 119, 120, 130, 132, 139, 141

Contents

For Mandy

Introduction

'One of the advantages of staying in one place is that you get to know the world deeply. You get a very deep sense of human community and the human experience.' [1]

I MADE A PROMISE to myself back in 1976 when we bought our house in Chitterne that one day when I had the time I would look into the house history and find out why it is round. Then we had two more children and the youngest Mandy was born with a malformed heart, my father died and my mother came to live with us and life was pretty busy for a while. It wasn't until 2000 that I finally started investigating the history of our house. The three eldest girls moved out and Mandy's deteriorating condition meant that she was unable to work so her web skills were put to use making a website for the house history. [2]

Canner's 'History of Chitterne' notes first fired up my interest in the history of the whole village. I used it to fill in the background story of Chitterne on the house history site and gradually the village history took over, eventually dwarfing the original purpose of the site. Clearly two sites were needed. Fate stepped in when the Village Hall Committee wanted a website to publicise the new hall; I suggested a site for the whole village and they agreed. Mandy was drafted in again to create the new Chitterne website from my ideas and www.chitterne.com went live in September 2001. In the beginning there were pages on the village hall, introduction and location.

Later on we split the original Round House website into two: village history and house history. The village history was added to chitterne.com, leaving the house history where it was.

From the very beginning people far from Chitterne have responded to both websites by email with their questions and offers of more information, and my research has been much augmented in this way. That is the exciting thing about the new technologies; interaction is so easy and quick. However, not everyone has a computer or wants one and there is something to be said for being able to read the words on paper in a book.

That is just one of the reasons for writing this book. There have also been hints that a book on Chitterne's history was needed. But for a long time I ignored them and thought, 'Who am I to write this book? I am an incomer, only lived here for 30 years; there are others who have greater claim to authorship, whose families have been here for generations...' and so on. Then I thought, 'maybe an objective view is the best way to see all that Chitterne has to offer, maybe I could do it', but still I tucked the idea away for later.

Fate intervened again, as it often will if you drag your feet. My daughter Mandy died, leaving her wonderful legacy of the two websites, and suddenly I had a lot of free time.

So here I am. Committed to sharing what I have discovered so far about Chitterne with anyone who is interested, and specially those who prefer the written page to the screen. That is not to say that this book is merely a print-out of my village history on the web, there is much more besides, but it could never be a definitive history of Chitterne as there is still so much more to discover.

Acknowledgements

I am indebted to my husband Dave, who has given me the time and space to write as well as the benefit of his computer expertise. To John Chandler who believed I could do this and to Diana Sanders who has painstakingly checked over my grammar. Any mistakes in the narrative are mine alone. Lastly, thank you to all the people listed below who have helped with the content of this book.

Pete Ash	Dave Bamford	The late James Carter
Peter Ashley	Maggie Bird at Met.	Elizabeth Chadwick
Fred and Kathleen Babey	Archives	Graham and Linda Dean
The late Bert Bailey	Dave Bridgen	Richard Essberger

David Feltham and Michael
  Holmes
Ray Feltham
Victor and Alan Feltham
Jack Field at Dewey
  Museum
Kay Findley
Roger Foyle
Rod Fripp
Ernie and Jeanne George
Arthur and Sarah Gooch
Connie Gorry
Roy and Julianna Grant
Alwyn Hardy at Dewey
  Museum
Lorna Haycock at WANHS
Steve Hobbs at WSRO

Sally Hudson
Pam Jones
Katy Jordan
Catherine Koppana
Mark Lockyer
Emmanuelle Longuepee
The late Percy Maidment
  and Ivy
Ken Michell
Mike Moody
Max Newell
Max Newman
Cheryl Nicol
Gillian Nolan
Nathan North
Vanessa Parker
Eric Peddle at Dewey

Museum
Ray and Freda Poolman
Robert and Virginia Pryor
Pat Ricketts
Joan Robertson
Sandy Sanders
Linda Saunders
Dorothy Sheppard
Michael Sheppard
Veronica Smedley
Alan Sprack
Ken Titt
Laurie Wallis
Liz Wallis-Long
Pauline White
Bill Windsor

Chitterne School c.1877. Henrietta Titt, William Brown and Sarah Brown are the three adults in the back row. Henrietta was the mother of Harold Nelson Dewey, who became a headmaster in Warminster.

The Where, How, Why and What of Chitterne

Where is Chitterne?

Edith Olivier: 'an Eternity lying in an Infinity.'

C HITTERNE is a small Wiltshire village that nestles in the folds of an area of chalk upland in Southern England known as the Salisbury Plain. It is on the easternmost edge of the administrative district of West Wiltshire bordering Salisbury district to the east and Kennet to the north. The nearest town is Warminster, 8 miles away. The villages of Codford lie 3 miles south, Tilshead 3½ miles north and Shrewton 5 miles east.

The Salisbury Plain is the largest area of uncultivated chalk upland in Europe. The vastness, the huge overpowering sky and the seemingly endless tracts of rolling downland give an overwhelming feeling of space and freedom. The Plain is criss-crossed by ancient trackways and overlaid by signs of human habitation and movement from time immemorial, all adding to the ancient open atmosphere that pervades this area of England.

39,000 hectares of the Plain is owned by the Ministry of Defence (MoD) and is known as the Salisbury Plain Training Area (SPTA). It has been used for the training of troops since 1897 and as a result has not been farmed intensively for many years. Imagine then, this huge area of chalk downs, a large chunk of it (38km by 14km) left in its natural state, except for the odd tank track, for 100 years; the scarp slope lies 9 miles to the north and west; the dip slope is dissected by the rivers

Cultivated downland near Chitterne.

Wylye and Avon that meet in the city of Salisbury 17 miles to the south-east; Chitterne village sits astride a winterbourne, the Chitterne Brook, a tributary of the River Wylye with its source at Imber, on the dip slope and in the midst of this untamed chalkland; an island of habitation in a sea of wilderness.

In the immediate environment of the village the land has been cultivated for centuries, and no signs remain of previous farming practices. Even so there can be no doubt that people have lived here for many, many years. For there exist countless examples of earlier existences in the areas just beyond the tamed landscape, on the land owned by the MoD. Their ownership has helped to ensure the survival of many historical monuments and trackways that would otherwise have been obliterated by deep ploughing.

> In Places entire fossilised landscapes survive, containing barrow cemeteries, 'Celtic' fields and linear boundaries and Romano-British settlements, all preserved as up-standing earthworks in a way that cannot be matched anywhere else in lowland Europe.[3]

Chitterne is one of few centres of habitation on the Plain proper. Imber, already mentioned, is no more, having been taken over by the military, Tilshead and Shrewton are the only others.

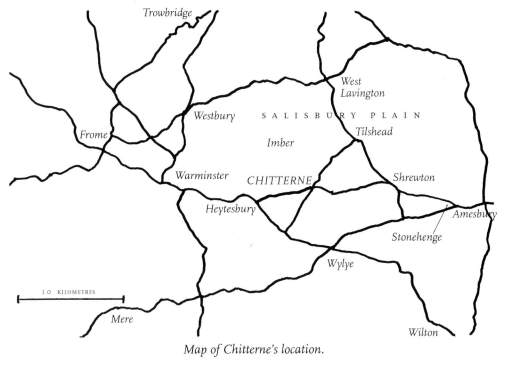

Map of Chitterne's location.

How did Chitterne come to be?

It is not possible to say when Chitterne was first settled, for unlike the nearby deserted sites at Knook and Chapperton Down, any relics from earlier habitations have been destroyed or lie buried beneath later buildings. At a guess, and it has to be a guess, Chitterne has been inhabited since the water table lowered sufficiently for people to settle near the winterbourne, known locally as the 'Cut' but properly called the Chitterne Brook.

The area had certainly been settled for many years by Anglo Saxon times when Chitterne had two settlements, but by the time of the Norman takeover three English, held it, Azor, Chenvin and Wulfwen, of whom more later. After the Norman conquest in 1066 Chitterne was held by another Englishman, Edward of Salisbury.

A settlement near Breakheart Hill may have been wiped out by the Black Death as, under the Normans, Chitterne again became two manors, Chitterne All Saints and Chitterne St Mary, or Upper Chitterne and Lower Chitterne. The two parishes were adjacent; the original boundary between them followed the middle of Bidden Lane (Shrewton Road). So those folks living on one side could just cross the lane into their neighbouring parish, whose inhabitants they considered 'furriners.' Nevertheless, for at least 500 years, the two parishes existed side by side, each with its own church and vicar, and flourished.

The combining of the two little villages started in 1819, when the ecclesiastical parishes of Chitterne All Saints and Chitterne St Mary were united under one vicar, although the actual deed did not become effective legally until 1914. By the mid 19th century neither of the two churches could hold the congregation, the combined population having reached 800, and besides, folk became confused as to which church to attend of a Sunday. A new much larger church was built in 1861 to replace the two small churches, but soon afterwards the population started to dwindle to the less than 300 souls who live here today.

On 17th January, 1907, by order of the Local Government Board the two old parishes became the civil parish of Chitterne.

Why Chitterne?

Where does the name Chitterne come from? There are several ideas but no one really knows. If the theory that the area has been inhabited for thousands of years is true, then the place must have had a name for that long, if only in spoken language.

The earliest written version, almost 1000 years old, found in the Domesday Book, is 'Chetre,' possibly derived from Cheltre/Celtre, meaning a place of refuge. That makes sense for a cluster of dwellings in a shallow cleft of the inhospitable and wild chalk upland of Salisbury Plain. But we must not forget that the Norman compilers of the Domesday Book may have misinterpreted the Saxon names, or put a 'Norman' bias on what they were hearing. We have no way of knowing how true to the original name the compiler of the Chitterne section was.

Over the following centuries many variations on the name appeared, such as: Cettra; Cetera; Cettre; Setre; Cetter; Chytterne; Chuterne; Chilterne; Chetterne; Chiltern; Chitturne. By the end of the 17th century Chittern or Chitterne became the usual name of the village.

It has also been suggested that the first part 'Chitt' may be a personal name: 'Cyta' or 'Kite,' there is a hill in the parish called Kite Hill, or British 'ceto' meaning 'wood.' The second element 'erne' may be from the Old English 'aern' meaning a store or house, as in 'barn' which means 'barley house' (ber-aern). Other villages in Wiltshire have the same name ending, for example: Colerne, which means a house or store for charcoal, or Potterne a house where pots were made or stored. Put the two parts together and Chitterne might mean 'Kite's house' or 'house in the wood.'

What has made Chitterne the Village it is?

The character of the village has been shaped by where it is, who owned it and what use they made of it. We have already looked at the isolated position of Chitterne in a previous paragraph. Geographically it is still isolated but nowadays with our modern communications and networks of roads, though we may grumble about the lack of public transport, we scarcely consider it so. But in the past that isolation had a profound effect on the people who lived here, because as the outside world moved on Chitterne was sometimes left behind.

Under the ownership of Lacock Abbey and Bradenstoke Priory in the middle ages Chitterne acquired a certain grandeur that sets it slightly apart from other Plain villages. The village was once much larger and more wealthy than it is now. When agriculture was its mainstay Chitterne was larger than Shrewton, Maddington and Tilshead, and more valuable to the nuns than Lacock itself. The majority of the villagers were employed by farmers, now very few residents work on the land. After the end of the 19th century when farming was becoming less profitable, the military stepped into the breach and bought up much of the agricultural land. The resulting influence on Chitterne's surroundings cannot be underestimated. We will be looking at the owners, farming and the military in later chapters.

How did Chitterne's isolated position affect the people who lived here? It meant that the inhabitants were mostly self-sufficient and remained stuck in the old ways of life longer, untouched by outside influences. It took longer for new inventions to be adopted. Horses were used for farm work until World War II, there was no mains water until the 1960s and no electricity until 1937. Even today (2007) we have no street lighting, no mains drainage, no piped gas and no mobile phone signal.

Customs continued in Chitterne that had long been forgotten elsewhere. For instance at the beginning of the 20th century villagers still curtseyed or touched their forelock when the owner of Chitterne House rode by, and the schoolchildren bowed and curtseyed to their teachers. The villagers, who still used 'thee' and 'thou' and the old English plural of house, 'housen,' in everyday speech, spoke 'Broad Wiltshire'. Mr Brown the schoolteacher said in 1893:

> What is a matter of every day observation in a town, one can give no conception of here, except by use of word pictures. The nearest railway station is at Codford, 3½ miles off, and many of the bigger boys and girls have never seen a train. What would a Londoner think of having to go eight miles to see coal gas burning?[4]

Young people were particularly stifled by the isolation. The only work available to school leavers was farm work as Chitterne was too far from the nearest town to walk there. Mr Brown: 'All the brightest boys look forward to getting away to the towns at the very first opportunity. No young fellow of energy will stay.'

Gradually the young people left, the population dwindled, eventually the farms mechanised and Chitterne became, for the most part, a village where the residents work elsewhere. There is a glimmer on the horizon: the revolution in electronic communications heralds the possibility that Chitterne might become a village of homeworkers, who knows? The cycle may turn full circle once more.

Chitterne All Saints from the Clump.

The Lords of the Manors

*A landlord who held land as a tenant of the Crown, or directly of the Crown, over
which he had full jurisdiction.*

THE EARLIEST RECORDS concerning ownership of Chitterne are to be found
in the Domesday Survey of 1086, made for William the Conqueror. According to this survey in pre-Norman times what is now the village of Chitterne was
then three settlements, held by three English, Azor, Chenvin and Wulfwen. These
settlements were not yet called manors, that would come later with the Normans
and their feudal system.

Azor was a housecarl of King Edward the Confessor; he held the largest of the
three parts of Chitterne. All Azor's lands and those of his men reverted to King
William after 1066 and by the time of the Domesday Survey they were held by
Edward of Salisbury.

Chenvin is a mysterious character, little is known of him but Edward of Salisbury also held his portion of Chitterne in 1086.

Wulfwen (or Ulwen) was one of the very few wealthy Englishwomen recorded
in Domesday as holding lands before 1066. Her lands stretched from Middlesex,
across Buckinghamshire, Wiltshire and Somerset to Dorset, a total of 65 hides, all
later held by Edward of Salisbury and, by 1086, this part of Chitterne was held for
Edward by Robert. This was the smallest portion of the three.

Therefore by 1086 Edward and Robert held what had previously been three
parts. This may have been the origin of the two Chitterne manors, and Edward was
probably the first Lord of the Manors, but who was he?

There is not a clear answer to the last question. What we do know is that
Edward of Salisbury was an Englishman of unknown parentage, who may have had

a connection with Wulfwen, and he held Chitterne at the time of the Domesday Survey. It was unusual for an Englishman to have survived the Norman invasion and to have been granted such a large area of southern England. Clearly Edward of Salisbury was a very important man. He was made Sheriff of Wiltshire and, possibly as early as 1170, had a castle at Old Sarum. In those days sherriffs derived their power directly from the king; they were the king's representatives in each shire. It was at Edward's castle that King William gathered all his faithful men together and had them swear oaths of allegiance to him in 1086.

Edward's son, Walter, gave some of his Chitterne lands including St Andrew's Chapel and Manor Farm to The Priory of Bradenstoke, which he founded in 1142. So the Prior of Bradenstoke became a landholder in Chitterne and Lord of the greater manor.

The lesser manor of Chitterne continued to be held by and passed down the family. From Walter's son Patrick, who was created Earl of Salisbury by Matilda in c.1149 as a reward for supporting her against Stephen, and later murdered by Guy de Lusignan; to Patrick's son William, the second Earl, who died leaving one daughter, Ela. Ela was eight when her father died in 1196 and she became Countess of Salisbury and heir to all her father's lands, including part of Chitterne. King Richard took her under his wing and soon betrothed her to one of his half-brothers, William Longespé, who then became Earl of Salisbury in her right. The couple had eight children, four girls and four boys. William was present at the signing of the Magna Carta in 1216 and the copy that is held in Salisbury Cathedral is said to have belonged to him. Ela and William laid a foundation stone each for the new cathedral being built at Salisbury in 1220. William went on a crusade and was away so long that many thought he had perished but Ela believed he was still alive and would return. However, after a feast to celebrate his safe return in 1226, he was suddenly taken ill and died; some thought he had been poisoned. He was the first to be buried in the partially-built cathedral, where his tomb can be seen to this day. Ela founded Lacock Abbey in his memory in 1229, became a nun there and later Abbess. She died in 1261 and is buried at Lacock.

In a similar way to the donation of part of Chitterne to Bradenstoke Priory by her ancestor Walter, Ela and her son, William Longespé II, gave all their lands at Chitterne to Lacock Abbey during 1246 and 1247. This gift ended the tenure of the Earls of Salisbury in Chitterne and the Abbess of Lacock now became Lord of the Manor alongside the Prior of Bradenstoke. It became usual for the land to be further sub-divided and sub-let to under tenants by indentures for lives, for years, or for years determined upon lives, usually three lives. One of the principal tenants under the Norman Earls of Salisbury was Roger Sifrewast[5] and under the Abbess of Lacock, the Morgan family.

The nuns of Lacock, the Prior of Bradenstoke and the College De Vaux[6] continued to benefit from the produce of their lands in Chitterne until King Henry VIII's dissolution of the monastic institutions. Lacock Abbey was finally dissolved in 1539. The nuns had prevented an earlier threat of dissolution by paying a fine of £300 to the king in 1537.[7] However, King Henry prevailed and the Chitterne lands were taken back by him and redistributed.

King Henry granted the Manor of Chitterne All Saints to John Williams and Anthony Stringer,[8] but as happened in several other institutions, members of the last Abbess of Lacock's family acquired some of the land, namely the Temys[9] family and the Manor of Chitterne All Saints. For John Williams and Anthony Stringer sold the manor to Thomas Temys for £207.14s. in 1545:[10]

> . . . all that our Manor of Chitterne in the County of Wilts with all and every its Richs
> members and appurtenances lately belonging to the Monastery of Bradenstoke in the
> said County . . . to have hold and enjoy the aforesaid Manner (sic) and the aforesaid
> Chapell of Chittern . . . dated the 25th day of Prille (April) in the yeare of the Reign of
> King Henry the 8th the 35th . . . [11]

Thomas Temys was the brother of Joan Temys, the last abbess of Lacock. Thomas Temys' son John inherited and his daughter Ann married William Jordan of Whitley, near Calne, Wiltshire who bought the manor from Ann's brother John Temys in 1580 for £440.

William Jordan was a wealthy man who gave £25 towards the fund for the protection of the country against the armada in 1588. His son and heir was Sir William Jordan who studied at Merton College, Oxford, obtained a BA in 1582-3 and was a student of Middle Temple in 1584. Sir William married twice, his son and heir, William, was born to his second wife in Chitterne about 1615. This third William was not so wealthy as his father or his grandfather; he borrowed £1000 from his mother in 1635, much of which he still owed at her death. Consequently in 1662 he sold the Manor of Chitterne All Saints to John Giles of Fisherton Delamere[12]

John Giles (or Gyles), the new Lord of the Manor of Chitterne All Saints also owned lands in Kingston Deverill. He died in 1669 and there was a stone memorial to him in the chantry chapel of old All Saints Church. His son, Benjamin Giles, of whom we know nothing, inherited his Chitterne farms and lands. However Benjamin's son, also Benjamin, lived here in Chitterne and, like his grandfather, was commemorated by a stone in All Saints Church when he died in 1710. It appears that when he wrote his will in 1709 he had no sons to inherit his Chitterne lands, but that he was hopeful of producing a son before he died. If he failed his estate was to be held in trust and the proceeds to be shared between his daughter, Dorothea, and his nephews.[13]

After the death of the second Benjamin Giles the Manor of Chitterne All Saints was acquired by John Holder, about whom we know nothing. But Paul Methuen of Corsham bought the Manor of Chitterne All Saints from John Holder in 1771.[14] Paul Methuen already owned the Manor of Chitterne St Mary.

The Methuens owed their wealth to an ancestor, Paul Methwin, who made a fortune from cloth in the reign of King Charles I. Paul Methuen of Corsham, lord of both manors in Chitterne, was the second cousin and heir of Sir Paul Methuen, who had been an illustrious statesman, rising to be comptroller of King George I's household, but who had died unmarried in 1757. Paul Methuen inherited considerable estates and many valuable works of art from Sir Paul and bought Corsham House to house the latter.[15]

Successive Methuen Lords of the Manor built up their portfolio of land and stock in both Chitternes, until they owned 3470 acres and a large flock of sheep. We will meet them again later in Chitterne St Mary.

Meanwhile the Michell family from Calston, near Calne, Wiltshire, were establishing themselves in Chitterne All Saints. Although not technically Lords of the Manor yet they were an extremely influential family in Chitterne and must be included here. Edward Michell's wife was Joan Danvers, niece of Sir John Danvers, the regicide, whose estates, which included Chitterne, were re-distributed by Act of Parliament in 1661 following his death in 1654. This is possibly how the Michell family came to be in Chitterne but there was yet another connection with the village. John Temys of Rood Ashton, great great grandfather of Thomas Temys who bought the Manor of Chitterne All Saints, married Mary the daughter of John Michell of Calston.[16]

The Michells are thought to have had Chitterne House built about 1680. Later they also owned the Mansion House[17] that once stood opposite the Village Hall. They purchased from it from Paul Methuen in 1775/6, but later it was demolished.

Edward Michell left a bequest for the Second Poor of Chitterne All Saints, to be distributed annually on St Thomas's Day. Charles Michell, a London merchant, who died in 1704 and is buried in All Saints graveyard, succeeded him. Charles's heir Christopher Michell and his wife Anne produced nine children, among them Commodore Matthew Michell, MP for Westbury; Thomas Michell, Rector of Graffham, Sussex; Robert Michell of Lincoln's Inn; Francis Michell a clerk in Chancery and Edward Michell who died at Fort St George in the East Indies. All the family are remembered on memorials now on the walls in Chitterne Church, and all except for Edward who is buried in the East Indies, are buried in the family vault in All Saints graveyard.[18]

Commodore Matthew Michell died in 1752 aged only 42 years, leaving a son, Matthew 14 months and a daughter Anne, three months old. Matthew Michell, son of Matthew the Commodore, and Robert, son of Thomas the Rector carried on the family involvement in Chitterne. Matthew Michell, a banker, who lived in London, and had also inherited the Hengar estate in Cornwall on the death of a cousin in 1786,[19] held the Mansion House at Chitterne. He bought Chitterne All Saints Manor, next door to his Mansion House, from Paul Cobb Methuen, son of Paul Methuen of Corsham, in 1815. Thus the two estates became as one and Matthew Michell became Lord of the Manor of Chitterne All Saints until his death in 1817. Robert Michell owned Chitterne House, the Gate House and 1400 acres of land on the other side of the road.

The Commodore Matthew Michell's daughter Anne, who married Sir Richard Onslow, inherited the estates in Cornwall and Chitterne after the death of her sister-in-law Louisa. Their son Sir Henry Onslow became Lord of the Manor of Chitterne All Saints on the death of Sir Richard in 1837. Sir Henry died in 1853 and is buried in All Saints graveyard in the Onslow-Michell tomb, but he did not live here, Manor Farm was leased to tenants.[20] He and his descendants lived in Cornwall.

Sir William Wallace Rhoderic Onslow lived in St Tudy, Cornwall when he was Lord of the Manor of Chitterne All Saints. Under his lordship the manor was offered for sale in 1895/6 and purchased by John Collins of Devon, just as times were beginning to change.

The old feudal ways were gradually giving way to a different way of living. In 1907 the two parishes became one and the old names of All Saints and St Mary disappeared except for the full name of the church, Chitterne All Saints' cum St

Chitterne St Mary from the Clump.

Mary's, which was generally shortened to Chitterne All Saints. The word 'manor' slowly came to refer solely to the manor house.

John Collins was not a remote figure as the Onslows had been; he was a farmer who lived in the village in Manor Farmhouse. His son Charles Collins worked along-side him and together they improved the farm, while Charles' sisters, Sarah and Eliza, supported the community. All three remained single. The Misses Collins, as the villagers knew them, hosted garden parties and fetes and encouraged the school-children, the Sunday schoolchildren and the church choir until the 1930s. Charles Collins died in 1937 at the time when the military were buying up more land on the Salisbury Plain.

By 1937 the War Department had bought the Chitterne Farm complex which included Chitterne Lodge and stables, Manor Farm, Elm Farm, Middle Barn, New House Farm, all the field barn settlements and many farmworker's cottages in the village itself. All Saints' Manor had a new Lord, the War Department, as it was styled then, later the Ministry of Defence. The WD leased out the farms and the land on the fringes of their training area to local farmers. Today, as the largest landowner in the area, the MoD remains Lord of the Manor.

In Chitterne St Mary, where the church held a good deal of the land, successive members of the Paulet family were Lords of the Manor. Starting with Henry Paulet, third son of the 4th Marquis of Winchester, in the early 17th century.

The family were royalists based in Hampshire who rose to prominence in Tudor times when William Paulet, the first Marquis of Winchester, was Lord Treasurer of England for 22 years. The following century their mansion at Basing had been demolished on Oliver Cromwell's orders and the family decanted to Amport, Hampshire. It was during Henry Paulet's time as Lord of the Manor that clay digging at Clay Pits on Chitterne St Mary Down was sanctioned for the manufacture of clay pipes at Amesbury.[21] Francis Paulet who kept a flock of sheep in Chitterne succeeded Henry in 1672 as Lord.[22] In 1696 Norton Paulet of Rotherfield, Hampshire became Lord of the Manor until 1741 and his son Norton Paulet, of Amport who sold the manor to Paul Methuen in 1758, followed him.[23]

Paul Methuen of Corsham bought the Manor of Chitterne St Mary from the Paulets in 1758 and, as we have seen earlier, the Manor of Chitterne All Saints in 1771. Paul Methuen's son, Paul Cobb Methuen, inherited both manors on his father's death in 1795 and added Samuel Biggs' farm in Chitterne St Mary, which he bought for £5750 in 1798. Just before his death in 1816 he sold Manor Farm, Chitterne All Saints to Matthew Michell. His son, Paul Methuen, a Wiltshire Member of Parliament and subsequently 1st Baron Methuen of Corsham, inherited but sold all the family's remaining estates in Chitterne, including the Manor of Chitterne St Mary to the trustees of the late Walter Long for £70,000 in 1830.[24]

A South Wraxall branch of the dispersed Long family was Lord of the Manor of Chitterne from 1830 until World War 1. They were connected to the Temys and Michell families who we encountered earlier, by virtue of holding an estate at Rood Ashton, near Trowbridge, Wiltshire, once held by John Temys.

Walter Long was the first member of the family to hold the lordship of Chitterne St Mary Manor, and was principal landowner in Chitterne All Saints; although not lord of the latter, he was treated as such by the villagers. The estate briefly passed to his son, Richard Penruddocke Long, in 1867 and subsequently his grandson, Walter Hume Long, in 1875.

Although none of the family lived here in Chitterne, the Longs continued the family's tradition of responsible lordship of the various Manors they held. Besides bequests of land and money to the communities, food and fuel was distributed to the poor on a regular basis and tenant houses were upgraded.

He (Walter Hume Long) would have a ton of coal brought from Radstock, hauled free by the farmers, and sell it to the villagers for 6d. a hundredweight.[25]

Walter Long gave the land for the village school in 1840 [26] and for the new church in 1861. He also gave £200 towards the cost of building the church.

Walter Long's grandson, Walter Hume Long of Rood Ashton, was the last of the old-style Lords of the Manor; the benevolent father figure who was generous to his tenants and appeared on important occasions. He followed a family tradition and became the conservative Member of Parliament for the Westbury constituency, serving as President of the Board of Trade and First Lord of the Admiralty during his 41 years as M.P., and

Walter Hume Long M.P.

later he was created 1st Viscount Wraxall. He succeeded to the estates in Chitterne upon his father's death in 1875, and mortgaged some of the properties prior to his marriage in 1878 to Lady Dorothy Blanche Boyle, daughter of the Earl of Cork and Overy.[27] Towards the end of the century Lord Long put some of the houses he owned in Chitterne up for sale, these included The White Hart Inn, The King's Head, The Grange, the Old Malthouse, The Round House, Bridge Cottage and several other cottages.[28]

Almost 20 years later Walter Hume Long found it uneconomic for one person to hold many large estates, with Lloyd George's new government policy on land tax,[29] so he sold most of them including his remaining estates at Chitterne, which were subsequently divided into smaller lots and sold again, some to the presently occupying tenants. The occupying tenants of The Manor, the Wallis family, purchased the house and farm in Chitterne St Mary from Walter Hume Long. Descendants of the Wallis family still live in The Manor today.[30]

Praying and Learning

THE WRITINGS of John Thomas Canner, vicar of Chitterne 1904-1925, prompted the first forays I made into the history of the village. Being a man of the cloth, and with access to church records, his notes were biased towards the church and its history. His research informs this chapter and I am indebted to him and his daughter Neva Canner for leaving such a valuable resource to the village.

The earliest mention of a religious building in Chitterne is of St Andrew's Chapel, which sadly no longer exists. It stood near The Gate House in the days when the family of the later Earls of Salisbury were lords of the manor. Some stone

Gated entrance to the site of St Andrew's Chapel.

coffins were unearthed behind the old gabled outhouse on The Gate House site and this is where the chapel is thought to have stood.[31] Walter, son of Edward the sheriff of Wiltshire, gave the chapel to Bradenstoke Priory, when he founded the priory in 1142. The priory of Bradenstoke, near Lyneham in north Wiltshire, was dedicated to the Blessed Virgin Mary and its inmates were canons of the order of St Augustine. In 1341 their chapel in Chitterne was valued at £3.3s.4d; the priory had besides: one carucate of land, pasture and a dovehouse here, valued at £1.6s.8d.[32]

Before the 14th century there were two churches in Chitterne, one for each parish: Chitterne All Saints and Chitterne St Mary. We know this because the advowson of Chitterne All Saints and 17 acres of its glebe land were bought for 120 marks in 1268 by the Dean and Chapter of Salisbury on the instructions of the executor the will of Giles de Bridport, Bishop of Salisbury. The income derived from this purchase in Chitterne was to be collected by the warden and scholars of the College de Vaux in Salisbury, founded by Giles de Bridport.[33] And also, the Dean and Chapter of Salisbury Cathedral held the rectory of Chitterne St Mary before 1291 when it was rated, with the Vicarage, at £6.13s.4d annually. We have lists of the incumbents dating from 1306 for All Saints and 1319 for St Mary, but the two stone-built structures that preceded the present church date from the 15th century. Both were demolished, except for their chancels, in 1861 and much of the material used to build the church that exists today, Chitterne All Saints with St Mary's.

The old Chitterne All Saints Church was sited to the north of the present church and on the other side of Chitterne Brook. It was a small building with a well-proportioned tower at the west end holding three bells. The chancel was separated from the nave by a plain pointed arch without columns and the ancient font is now in the present church. There were no side aisles but a small chantry chapel on the northern side founded in 1529 by Edward Morgan, nephew of John Morgan senior, tenant of the Abbess of Lacock; and an addition made by the Michell family to serve as pew and mausoleum in 1775. The latter was originally sited above ground, but during the demolition of the church it was re-sited below ground on the same spot and now marks the site of the former church in the graveyard of All Saints. The chancel of All Saints was initially kept as a mortuary chapel following the destruction of the church, but it was later found to be superfluous to requirements and demolished in 1877. There were some encaustic tiles in the chancel floor, which helped to date the building, bearing the arms of Simon Sydenham, Dean of Salisbury 1418-1431 and William Alnewyke, Archdeacon of Salisbury 1420-1426. The Dean

All Saints Church painted by John Buckler c.1805. The nave was demolished in 1861 and the chancel in 1877.

and Chapter of Salisbury were alternative patrons of the living. Part of a tile bearing the arms of Simon Sydenham was unearthed in All Saints graveyard when a grave was being dug on 29th June 1910.

All Saints Church held seven monuments to the Michell family, most of which are now in the present church vestibule, and their mausoleum held one more, now similarly displayed. There were two gravestones dating from the 17th and 18th centuries in the chantry chapel to the Giles family, who once owned Manor Farm, and another of 1783 in the aisle that commemorated William Lawes, former churchwarden of Chitterne All Saints.

The Michell family had two separate vaults at All Saints Church. The Onslow-Michell vault was below ground in the chancel. The Chitterne House Michells vault was housed in a tomb within their large elevated pew in the body of the church. The tomb contained eleven coffins each covered in crimson velvet. Thus the living members of the family sat in the company of their deceased forbears as they worshipped. These eleven coffins were relocated underground upon the destruction of the church in 1861. When the underground vault was being dug the gravediggers noticed, at a

St Mary's Church painted by John Buckler c.1805. The nave was demolished in 1861. In the background is the Manor complete with the wing that was later removed.

depth of 11 feet (3.35m), that the earth had been disturbed earlier. They found the shape of a man's body cut into the chalk that contained the bones of a very tall man. A piece of oak about 2 inches (5cm) thick had been placed over the body, without identification, in an earth to earth burial. As previously stated the Michell vault still exists, roughly in the middle of All saints graveyard, with its contents of eleven members of the Michell family, and nearby one unidentified tall man.

The site of the former Church of Chitterne St Mary is more obvious since the chancel still remains in the centre of St Mary's graveyard. It was kept, like the chancel of All Saints, as a mortuary chapel and it is still used for that purpose and occasionally for church services. St Mary's Church was even smaller than All Saints Church and was almost completely hidden from the village road by the old Tithe Barn, which has since been demolished. It had a low turret over the south porch, no side aisles, but a small chantry chapel on the north side. The chancel was separated from the nave by a low arch with open Gothic screenwork and quatrefoils on each side. This screen is now to be seen in the present church. The font was old and plain.

The Ecclesiastical Commissioners keep St Mary's chancel in good repair and receive the tithes from St Mary's parish. To the north of the altar is part of a tomb with an ogee arch dating from about 1500. Originally there may have been four pillars supporting a band of tracery and a canopy over the tomb, which may have had figures lying on top; now there are only the two pillars. It must be the tomb of a wealthy person, but there is no clue as to who, it is a mystery.[34] On the chancel walls are murals to the memory of Samuel and Ann Biggs, Ann Sanders and John Sanders. In the chancel floor vicar John Dowland, one-year-old Charles Williams, son of a curate, and Elizabeth Morris are commemorated.

An Ogee tomb arch from c.1500 possibly removed from the old St Mary's Church before the demolition of the main building and re-sited inside St Mary's chancel by T.H.Wyatt.

There is another curious mystery attached to the burial of Elizabeth Morris of Mere under the floor of St Mary's Chancel. She was the widow of Jeremiah Morris and mother of Joseph Brown Morris, the curate of Chitterne St Mary 1808-15. He and his mother lodged at the Round House with Charlotte Folliott, herself a widow. Elizabeth was the daughter of a Mr Shurland, a senator of Barbados, and when she died in 1812 the entry of her death in the burial record is followed immediately by another entry for: 'Charles Morris, negro boy,' who was buried the following day. The grave of Elizabeth's negro boy is now unmarked, but in recent memory is known to have been just outside St Mary's graveyard beyond the kissing gate at the north-east corner, and marked by a small round boulder that has since disappeared.[35] Why the two deaths occurred so close together we do not know, we can only guess; newspaper reports of Elizabeth's death do not mention the boy.

Outside the chancel on the north and east facing walls are tablets to the

The chancel of St Mary's Church c.1450.

memory of the Wheeler family, innkeepers, and to the Huntley family, farmers. In the graveyard of St Mary's are three listed tombs: of William Ingram; William and Mary Wallis; and John and Mary Parham; farmers all three. In the north-east corner almost totally obscured by a yew tree is the tomb of Reverend Tovey, the source of yet another curious tale.

The Reverend Thomas Leach Tovey was curate of both parishes at Chitterne and must have been blessed with foresight. On 31st October 1842 he planted a yew tree in St Mary's churchyard in the presence of Rev. Johnson, vicar of Tilshead, saying that it would be a memorial of him when he was gone. On the very same day he was taken ill, and the next day he went to Salisbury for medical advice, where he died. His body was brought back to the same churchyard and on the 25th November 1842 he was buried near his tree, which indeed serves as his memorial, as to this day it is known as the Reverend Tovey's Tree.[36]

On completion of the new church of Chitterne All Saints with St Mary's it was discovered that it would be impossible to bury the dead in the surrounding land as newly dug graves quickly became waterlogged. So the old graveyards have continued in use ever since. Both are slightly larger than originally. All Saints graveyard was enlarged in the 19th century after a gift of land by Sir William Onslow.[37] St Mary's

All Saints cum St Mary's Church built 1861.

graveyard was added to in 1928 when Ushers Brewery donated some land formerly part of the King's Head plot.

Why was such a large new church built? For several reasons: the size of the population, which was almost 800 souls in mid 19th century; confusion over the venue for the services after the parishes of Chitterne All Saints and Chitterne St Mary were united under one vicar in 1819; and the state of repair of the two old churches.

Walter Long, Lord of the Manor at the time, gave a site more central for the combined parishes, which turned out to be rather damp as mentioned above. The foundation stone was laid by the Venerable Archdeacon MacDonald, vicar of Chitterne, on Tuesday 13th August, 1861, in front of his curate: George Richards, and his churchwardens: Henry Hitchcock, William Wallis, John Titt and Frederick Lavington. The architect was T.H.Wyatt and the builder Solomon Gayton. The building cost £2404 and was consecrated by the Bishop of Salisbury on 4th November 1862. George Richards was the first vicar of the new church. While the new church was being built

Norman font from All Saints Church with the font cover made by James Townsend in 1767.

other arrangements were made for holding services, weddings, christenings and funerals. For instance William Foyle and Thirza Polden were married on the 15th February 1862 in the parochial schoolroom, temporarily licensed for the purpose.

As mentioned earlier, building materials, the Michell monuments, a font and a screen came from the two old churches to be part of the new. Besides these there are two brass plates engraved with the Lord's Prayer and the Ten Commandments dating from 1788 in the new chancel that came from All Saints Church, as did the font, which is worth mentioning again. It is thought to be of Norman origin from its design, which is in two patterns cut alternately that do not match at the join. The oak cover was made in 1767 by James Townsend, for which he was paid £2.5s. Could this possibly be the Townsend who owned cottages at the Tilshead end of the village and gave his name to that section of Chitterne All Saints?

The five bells that hang in the bell-tower all come from the two old churches. Three of them are St Mary's old bells, the other two were recasts of the three old bells from All Saints, made in tune with the others in 1862, by G. Mears and Company of Whitechapel, London. One of the old St Mary's bells is very old indeed. It was cast by John Barbur of Salisbury who died in 1403, so it is at least 600 years old. The other two from St Mary's were cast by James Burroughs of Devizes in 1754 and bear the names of William Tinker and John Compton, churchwardens. There has always been a team of ringers in Chitterne who turn out for Sunday services, christenings, weddings and funerals and for celebrations. In past years it was the custom for the village bell ringers to ring in the New Year, and afterwards sit down to a sandwich supper provided by the landlord of the King's Head. Alfred Burt was Tower Captain in those days. More recently, under the captaincy of George Unsworth White, the bells rang out to celebrate the millennium.

The Hayward family, formerly of Chitterne House, donated the stained glass window at the end of the side aisle in 1919, in memory of those that gave their lives in World War 1. The lectern was given by the Feltham family in memory of Beryl Feltham who was church organist for many years and died in 1977. Paul Hopkins of Bristol installed the present organ in 1993.

Memorial window to the men who died in World War 1 donated by the Hayward family in 1919.

What of the incumbents of these three churches over the years? Most of them are simply names on a list but occasionally there is a story to tell. Jervase Bland was vicar of Chitterne All Saints 1660-1676 and also curate of Knook (a small village about 4 miles south-west of Chitterne). In 1667 he complained that no bible was provided at Knook as he had ordered; that the people did not come to his services there; and that the clerk was inefficient. At Heytesbury, a larger village nearby to Knook and also under his curacy, the minister gave communion to people before the day that had been appointed; none of the young were sent to be catechised;

and on arriving on the correct day to receive the churchwardens accounts and appoint new churchwardens he found the church locked and no one came, so no churchwardens were chosen. Even worse was to come, he said:

> They have also brought in strangers into the church in sermon time speaking aloud taking my words out of my mouth, repeating again that I said to my great disturbance making me end the sooner. I asked their names, nobody would tell me. Strangers they said they were and knew not their names though working in the parish. They struck my hat with boughs and threw it about the chancel so that when I came out of the pulpit I could not find my hat and therefore for the second time I crave for justice to be roused in this High Court at Salisbury to redress such intolerable abuses.

Perhaps the Rev. Bland lived up to his name when in the pulpit! The Reverend Tovey, he of the foresight, although in this case he seems to have lost the talent, suffered likewise in the 19th century. But at least the young men of Chitterne made their feelings known with more humour and in rhyme. This is what they sent to him:

> If you do not your sermons dock
> You'll surely lose one half your flock;
> For short ones we've been always used to,
> And to hear your long ones we don't chose to.
> At twelve o'clock our dinner is done,
> But you keep us in till after one;
> And in again we go at two;
> We've neither time to bolt or chew.
> We all intend going up the Lane,[38]
> Whether it's you or we to blame.
> To hear your sermons we're all minded
> If you were not so very long winded.

It is thanks to a later vicar of Chitterne, Rev. John Thomas Canner 1904-1925, that these priceless tales are preserved in the village. He was very interested in local history and recorded many such events in his notebook. One wonders what he

Rev. John Thomas Canner and family outside the Vicarage.

would have made of his successor, Rev. Arthur Clifford Hawkes 1926-1954. This gentleman must have had no problem keeping his congregation quiet and attentive, they would have been too curious to stay away, he was an eccentric. According to local lore he took services in his wellies, tied his dog-collar with a bootlace and kept a cockerel in a cage on his desk!

Music in the church was provided by dedicated organists. Abdon Polden played the church organ and sang in the choir for many years; he was succeeded by Beryl Feltham, his granddaughter, whose long service in that capacity is commemorated on a plaque fixed the back of the harmonium in the present church. The church choir consisted of adults and children, both boys and girls. Miss Feltham also led choir practice held on Wednesday evenings, and Miss Collins of Manor Farm was often there in a front pew listening and giving encouragement. In the summer she rewarded the choir and Sunday school pupils with a tea-party on her front lawn. At the tea-party Miss Collins handed out merit and attendance prizes of prayer books or bibles to the Sunday School, in the presence of the Sunday schoolteacher and the vicar. After Miss Collins' time the vicar hosted Church Sunday School parties at the Vicarage. There is no longer a choir at Chitterne.

Sunday Schools were held at the chapel as well as the church and every summer in either June or July the Sunday School teachers organised outings to the seaside for their pupils and mothers. The chapel outing was nearly always on a Wednesday to Southsea, and the church outing on a Friday to Bournemouth. The children saved up throughout the year towards their pocket money for the outing. At Sunday School Miss Feltham collected the church children's money and Mrs Maidment collected the chapel children's. Come the day of their outing all the children gathered near the church and climbed aboard one of Mr Cornelius' open-topped charabancs for an exciting trip to the sea.[39] Today Sunday School has been replaced by Sunday Club, for children aged 4 to 11 years, held every Sunday morning during school terms in the Village Hall.

Every Easter an Easter garden is built on a platform in the church beyond the screen. The platform is covered in wire and the children collect moss and flowers to place over the wire. There is a closed stone tomb on Good Friday and Saturday but on Easter Sunday the stone covering the opening to the tomb is secretly rolled away exposing the linens inside. This scene captures the imagination of the children. One enterprising village child in the 1960s tried to see who was doing the rolling

Church summer outing in Rev. J.T. Canner's time (1904 – 1925).

away by keeping watch from the top of the slide in the sportsfield, but without success.[40]

In recent years the annual Flower Festivals held in the church have been a major fundraiser for the maintenance of the church fabric. Pru Heaton-Ellis was the director for a number of years, and set the high standard which continues to date under the direction of Virginia Pryor and her dedicated band of helpers. The displays in the church, the open village gardens and the cream teas served in the hall attract a large number of visitors to the village over the Flower Festival weekend.

During the 1960s the parish of Chitterne was united with that of Tilshead under one vicar who lived in the vicarage at Tilshead. Chitterne's vicarage was sold.[41] About 30 years later Tilshead and Chitterne parishes were united with Shrewton and Orcheston under one vicar, and the vicar lived at Shrewton. Rev. Mike Fearn was the first incumbent of the group of four parishes; Rev. Sue Armitage, our current vicar, succeeded him.

Non-Conformity in Chitterne

Non-conformist meetings were being held in Chitterne in the 18th century. George Grant (1753-1840) was a dedicated Baptist and attended meetings in Chitterne. In 1801 his own house in Chitterne, occupied by his son John 'Shepherd' Grant (1779-1848), was registered as a meeting house for Baptist services.[42] By 1846 a chapel had been built but was held by the Wesleyan Methodists, however they were unable to 'work the cause' so far from Salisbury and the chapel was handed back to the Baptists.[43]

A Mrs. Grant was treasurer for the Chitterne Baptists in 1883, together with chairman Mr. S. King; Frank Mabbitt, secretary and William Ashley, Jacob Smith and Joseph Mabbitt, deacons. Baptisms were carried out at Corton, as there were no facilities at Chitterne; Herbert Smith, Elizabeth Mabbitt, John Smith, Emmanuel Stokes, Thomas Bendal, William Ashley and Frank Ashley were baptised. Individual conduct was considered of great importance and Baptists could be expelled for walking in a disorderly fashion.

In 1884 Chitterne Baptists agreed to be grouped with other churches at Shrewton and Tilshead and their numbers were increasing, Frank Poolman, Frank Feltham, Samuel Tilly, Job Grant, Charles Coles and Sarah Bundy joined. In 1888 Robert Hinton played the harmonium at the services, he was paid £1.10s. per year. The pastor was T. Allen Judd who was succeeded in 1889 by H.J. Smith. Also in

1889 Frank Maidment and his wife Rose were baptised and Frank was asked to be a deacon. Later that year he presided over meetings and started taking services. [44]

On 1st April 1903 a fire started in the thatched roof of the Baptist Chapel, after an evening meeting had been held there, and soon destroyed most of the building, only the schoolroom escaped. Most moveable objects were saved, but a new venue was needed and Farmer Wallis agreed to the Baptists using his malthouse for the summer. A site for the new chapel near the old one was given by Walter Long MP; it was prepared by chapel men who came after their day's work with their pikes, shovels and barrows to remove the chalk, and farmers sent horses and carts to take the chalk away to fill holes on their farms free. Mr

Chitterne Baptist Chapel harmonium player c.1880. Probably Robert Hinton.

L.C. Cook laid the foundation stone on the 4th November 1903. Mr. Burbidge, a director of Harrods in London, offered the interior of a congregational chapel he had purchased to furnish the new chapel, in memory of happy holidays he had spent in Chitterne at his brother's farm. A friend had some doors given to him from Potterne Church that he donated to the cause. A Mr. Deacon of Swindon gave the lamps for inside and out. The new chapel was opened almost exactly a year after the disastrous fire that destroyed the old one. [45]

Money for the new chapel was raised everywhere Frank Maidment preached as he relates in the Minute Book:

> The sacrifice of our friends was wonderful. One old friend at Imber about 80 (years old) did some little (jobs) for 2d or 3d and one day gave me 10s which he had saved to give a thankoffering to God for Spiritual help from sermons I had preached at Imber. A poor widow in our village gave me 2/6d one Sunday after Christmas as God had sent her some friends to help her. She was poor, only on Parish relief of 3s per week.

The Imber friend was only allowed 2s per week. In each case I said: 'I cannot take it,' both said 'you must, it's for God's House,' and I had many other cases like it.

The new building was not without problems. In March 1905 the chapel building fund was in deficit £275 which was finally paid off in 1910; chalk kept falling down the hillside behind the chapel, which constantly needed clearing, and by 1923 the chapel roof was in a bad state. Messrs Polden Brothers estimate of £67.17s.6d. for the repairs was accepted, and the Baptist Association loaned £50 free of interest towards the cost, but the debt had not been cleared by 1934.

The newly rebuilt Baptist Chapel c.1904. The gentleman with a moustache and straw boater in the back row is Frank Maidment.

Nevertheless, except for the war years, under the leadership of Frank Maidment the chapel thrived. The visiting committee visited the sick, a new organ was purchased in 1911 and a Young People's Meeting was introduced in 1919 on Tuesday Evenings.

As the century progressed there were fewer Candidates for baptism and attendance dwindled. After the death of Frank Maidment in 1952 Pastor Lawes became leader and the chapel eventually closed.

Learning

A fascinating in-depth interview with Beryl and Nora Feltham, by villager Mrs Nixon-Eckersall in 1975, has informed and shaped the following paragraphs about the village school. The Misses Feltham, as they were affectionately known, were involved with the school, Sunday school and church over many years. At the time of the interview they were aged 90 and 80 years respectively, and remembered life in Chitterne at the turn of the 20th century. I have used their memories of school-life at that time and covered the subsequent 60 years of the school's existence by interviewing pupils from the 1930s and 1960s.

Beryl, Esme and Nora Feltham pictured on the Rogation Day ramble 10 May 1969.

Chitterne School was built in 1840 on land near the village green, given by Lord of the Manor, Walter Long. The villagers themselves constructed the building, making the walls of cob,[46] the roof of slate, and a playground at the front surrounded by a wall with a gate. It had been agreed that it was to be used as a school during the day and a meeting place in the evenings for the Village Benefit Club. Mr. And Mrs. Fry were schoolmaster and schoolmistress in 1841;[47] Francis Child and his wife Mary Ann in 1851[48] and Annie Light was the schoolmistress in 1861.[49] William Brown and his wife Sarah took over in 1867 and stayed for 39 years.

In William Brown's time the building was divided into two rooms, one large and one small. The children were taught in three groups. The youngest, ranging in age from 4 to 9 years, in the small room and the other two groups shared the large room, divided by a folding screen. The small room had a gallery and four or five rows of tiered seats, with the oldest children sitting at the back. These children rested their slates, provided by themselves, on their knees, as there were no desks. In the larger room were two box desks with seats attached and some sloping desks with shelves underneath. The heating was by coke burned on tortoise stoves. They gave out a good heat but also awful fumes when the wind was blowing in a certain direction. There was no water laid on, so pupils and staff were obliged to go to a neighbouring cottage to wash their hands, to have a drink or to relieve themselves. Toilet facilities in the village were known as vaults, deep pits with a sheer drop, shared between several dwellings.

The impact that the school, and compulsory education from the 1870s, made on the isolated farming community can only be imagined. Most of the inhabitants were illiterate and old customs continued to be followed long after they had been forsaken in the towns. It was the custom for the schoolchildren to bow and curtsey to their teachers and superiors until well into the 20th century. Their speech was full of 'thees' and 'thous' and 'housen' instead of houses. Most of the children had never seen a train although the nearest station was at Codford only 3½ miles away.

School began at 9 am and finished at 4 pm. The school bell rang at 8.45 am, a valuable addition to the striking of the Church clock for villagers with no other way of telling the time. Children would arrive having eaten bread and lard for breakfast if they were lucky, nothing at all if not. Reading, writing and arithmetic were taught, a little history and geography, and the Vicar took Religious Instruction. Agriculture was a popular class subject with the boys and the girls learned needlework.[50] They practised traditional stitches on strips of calico and then unpicked them and started again. Punishment was standing in a corner or occasionally, the cane. School ended when a child reached 14 years of age, but those who passed the Fourth Standard could leave at 12.

School attendance was affected most at potato planting and harvesting times and often not all children of agricultural workers went to school. Sometimes they attended in relays, they might take it in turns to wear the only pair of boots to school while the rest stayed at home.[51] Elizabeth Stokes, born 1874, was the youngest of ten children, only she and her next eldest sister attended school. Her parents and brothers contributed a groat a week towards their education.[52]

Children from the field barn settlements would have to walk to school through all weathers, often along 18-inch deep rutted muddy tracks, and sometimes needed to be collected and brought to school in carts for the annual examinations.[53]

Despite all these drawbacks William Brown was a good, dedicated schoolmaster, now helped by his daughter Rosa, as Assistant Mistress. Eunice Grant was the school cleaner. In 1903 the Education Department report noted:

The work has been done with thoroughness and intelligence, and the progress and condition of the children are very satisfactory. The infants are being nicely taught, and they do their work brightly and well.[54]

Some good results were achieved under his headship. The Bazell family, who lived at Clump Farm, for instance, had thirteen children and all the boys won scholarships to Dauntsey's School (a public school at West Lavington). William said, of his boy pupils, that: 'No young fellow of energy will stay in Chitterne.' They didn't, there was nothing but farm work for them in the village, and for the girls, domestic service. Chitterne was too far away from a town to walk to work there and the nearest station in Codford, so most of those boys went away to live and became postmen, policemen or drivers, as did William's own son. [55]

Following Mr Brown's death in 1906, his wife Sarah and his daughter Rosa Polden resigned their positions as assistant teachers. Miss Beryl Feltham agreed to stand in for a short while, as she thought at the time, but she stayed for 43 years teaching the infants. Miss Watson was head teacher in the 1920s. At the end of every Autumn term just before Christmas, Miss Collins of Manor Farm arrived at school with a bag of shiny new pennies that she distributed to each child in turn, calling them all by name and wishing them a 'Merry Christmas.' In return the children sang carols to her accompanied by Miss Feltham at the piano.[56]

In the 1930s Mrs Taylor from Westbury was the head teacher, still helped by Miss Feltham. Mrs Taylor was said to be 'handy with the ruler'. In 1935, King George V's silver jubilee year, two children from the school, the eldest girl and eldest boy, planted two commemorative trees in Miss Awdry's paddock behind the church. A silver birch and a hornbeam, but sadly both trees died before the end of World War II.[57] Miss Royston took over as head from Mrs Taylor. Susie Found was the school cleaner for many years.

Every morning would start with prayers, followed by arithmetic, reading or writing. The children from the field barn settlements who had to walk 2 or 3 miles to school arrived about 10 o'clock and left again just after 1 o'clock to return home. At morning break milk and biscuits were available, the milk would have been kept warm near the tortoise stove that still provided the school's heat. Sometimes there was Horlicks made with hot milk. Most children went home to lunch and would return to study geography or history in the afternoon. By this time there was a block of school toilets, beyond the main building in the playground, with girls' toilets at one end and boys the other. Games such as 'Tinker Tailor Soldier Sailor Who Can Touch The Wall' were played in the small playground. On special occasions Miss Awdry, and later Mrs Maxton, of the Grange allowed the school to use their paddock behind the school.

Before the advent of 11+ examinations, children sat for a scholarship exam that might enable them to go on to grammar school at Trowbridge or Salisbury. But even if they passed the scholarship exam the cost of attending high school might be too great for their parents to afford, so only a few children went. Others attended the Avenue Secondary School in Warminster until they were 14.

The traditional help given on farms by schoolchildren at harvest time continued, indeed if the harvest was late special arrangements would be made by the farmers with the school for the children involved to be excused lessons until the crops were safely gathered in. [58]

Chitterne School c.1940. Back row: Tony Bailey; George Goodenough; Terry Gorry; Alan Feltham; Trevor Johns (evacuee); Richard Brown (evacuee); Alan Coates; John Bowler (evacuee); unknown; unknown. Second row: unknown; Norman Bowler (evacuee); David Feltham; Bernard George; unknown; Wilma Goodenough; unknown; unknown; Trixie Gorry; Sylvia Feltham; Mary Mould; unknown; John Williams; Maurice Cauchois (evacuee); Terry Wells. Third row: unknown; Winnie Johns (evacuee); Peggy Daniels; Pat Plumbley; unknown; Thelma Herrington; Ruby Mould; Ann Cruse; George Mould. Front row: unknown (evacuee); Bert Potter; Pip Poolman; Bobby Feltham; Ron Potter; Richard Feltham; Colin Gorry; Ray Poolman; Arthur Polden.

During the World War II school numbers were swelled by an influx of evacuees, about 20 or 30 extra children were accommodated in the village, wherever there was space or an empty dwelling. Some came with their mothers, some without. Some were from the Channel Islands, such as the Lecocq family on the Green. The others were all from the same area of London and knew each other. Evacuee Norman Bowler and his older brother John, from London stayed here with the Windsor family from 1940 – 1945. They attended school and, like the local boys, worked on farms in the school holidays:

> When we first arrived in Wiltshire the local children thought we were very strange with
> our London accents. They sized us up and there was a bit of a rumble and then we were
> quickly accepted. Then, when we went back to our parents, the kids in London took the
> mickey out of our country accents and we found it difficult to understand them. [59]

The experience gave Norman a lifelong love of the countryside. He still returns to see old friends and occasionally opens Chitterne Fete. No doubt Chitterne youngsters horizons were broadened too from contact with children who had grown up in such a different environment.

In 1954 the Headmistress was Mrs Burton and assistant mistress, Mrs Veale. The children were segregated at playtimes, there was a small playground behind the school used for play by the infant children only. The infant room could be accessed from the back of the building or from the large room. The juniors played in the playground at the front of the school. At the end of Autumn term the children were treated to a display of conjuring, ventriloquism and a Punch and Judy show by Mrs Veale's husband Mr Stafford Veale. Mr Veale's dummy, Rodney, presented each child with a candy bar. [60]

Miss Selby, who lived in Abdon Close, was Head Teacher in the 1960s. Miss Selby wore her hair swept back off her high forehead, sometimes wisps escaped when she was cross, but not often. The Infant teacher was Miss Smith from Westbury. Miss Smith was older and everyone's idea of a granny. She was plump with white fuzzy hair. Every child who left her class to move on to the junior one was given a small teddy bear type toy that she had made herself. Doris Windsor cleaned the school.

There were only two classes in the 1960s. The Infants in the small room and the Juniors in the large. The main door led to a porch, where coats and bags were hung, which then led into the large room. The school was still heated by tortoise stove. The toilet block was behind the school. The toilets were of the bucket type;

the buckets were emptied once a week. You only used them if you were desperate. All the children played together at playtime, and, as in earlier times the playground wall often featured in their games such as: 'L-O-N-D-O-N spells London.' 'Please Mr Crocodile may we cross the river?' was another favourite. At the side of the school next to Yew Tree Cottage the school rabbit and guinea pig were kept in hutches. Children walked home for lunch and mothers waited under the chestnut tree on the green for their children.

At assembly every morning the children marched in single file into the large room, there was no school bell, just someone calling: 'In time.' The children stood in line facing towards the church, to sing a hymn and hear Miss Selby talk. Then they gathered around Miss Selby's desk and listened while she read an extract from a Children's Bible. She started at the beginning and read a section each day until she reached the end, then started from the beginning again.Every Christmas the school performed a nativity play, always using the same script, and the authorised version of the bible.

In the junior class the desks, of the table type, were arranged around the edge of the room. Miss Selby was a good teacher and had no discipline problems; one of her cross looks was enough to bring a child back to attention. In 1965 one of the four leavers passed the 11+ examination, a remarkable result for such a small village school but even this success could not prevent the inevitable. The numbers of children were dwindling, from 17 to 13, and it was becoming obvious that the school was no longer viable.

Following a car accident Miss Smith worked only part-time, listening to children reading in the small room, and then she retired. Miss Selby taught the whole school in one class in the large room. The style of teaching changed and the children worked out of workbooks in the morning. There were three books: for reading, writing and mathematics. As long as you completed one section of each every day you could do the work in any order you liked and then take it up to the teacher's desk to join the queue to be marked. Sometimes a child would have to skip a section such as: measuring the playground, and it would be done later, perhaps after lunch. In the afternoon periods the children might play rounders in the sportsfield, listen to a history programme about dinosaurs on the radio, or do PE indoors. The school day ended with a story. Then the children put their chairs up on their desks 'for the cleaner.' Standing behind their desks, they sang, 'God be in my head,' before going home.

The fabric of the school slowly deteriorated; the playground tarmac became rough and weeds started to grow through it. It fell to Miss Selby to light the stove, and once, as she bent to the task, the flames blew back in her face singeing her hair and eyebrows. The children laughed at the sudden noise and flame, but not for long, as Miss Selby was furious with them.

At the end of Summer Term 1967 the school closed and most of the 13 remaining children went to Codford School but Diana Dean went to Steeple Langford School where Miss Selby was to take up a teaching post. Sadly Miss Selby died soon after, of an allergic reaction to vaccinations for a foreign holiday. She died in the United States and her body was brought back to England for burial.[61]

After the school's closure in July 1967 the building, still owned by the Long family, was used occasionally for village events. Lord Long gave it to the village and it was refurbished, with a new entrance hall and flush toilets in place of the old porch and a scullery added, leaving a main hall and a smaller room for committee meetings and such. The building was re-opened in 1970 as the Village Hall.

Chitterne School 1967. The last school photograph. Back row: Timmy Poolman; Paul Williams; Winnie Grant; David Williams; David ? Middle row: unknown; Diana Dean; Miss Smith; Miss Selby; Mrs Gorry; Lavinia Goodenough; Lougene Goodenough. Front row: Billy George; Nigel Gorry; unknown; unknown.

Tracks and Robbers

*'... by and by to bed, glad of the mistake because it seems, had we gone on as we
pretended, we must have lain on the plain all night.' Samuel Pepys*

I F SAMUEL PEPYS came back to Chitterne today he would be astounded not
only by the roads but by the traffic. And not only by the lack of horses, but by the
numbers of horseless vehicles that now pass through this once isolated village. For
nowadays one of our village roads, the B390, is part of a very popular route for
those travelling from the west wishing to join the A303/M3. The speed of traffic
through the village is the most talked about subject amongst present villagers, and
new remedies to slow it down are always being tried, the latest being mobile speed
camera units. But in ancient times there was a very different problem: which track
to take?

There were so many tracks across Salisbury Plain that it could prove extraor-
dinarily difficult to try and untangle them, but we are interested only in those that
affect Chitterne, and we must not be distracted by the immensity of the task.[62]
Perhaps here I should mention that there is no railway, canal or navigable river in
the village, and the only aircraft flying in the area are military.

For thousands of years the high points or ridgeways of the chalk hills and
downs of southern England provided many natural routes between settlements
and meeting places for the inhabitants who dwelt on the high plain. But once the
Plain had been deforested there was little to impede progress in any direction, hence
the proliferation of tracks. The most favoured routes are marked by barrows along
the way, such as Bowl's Barrow.

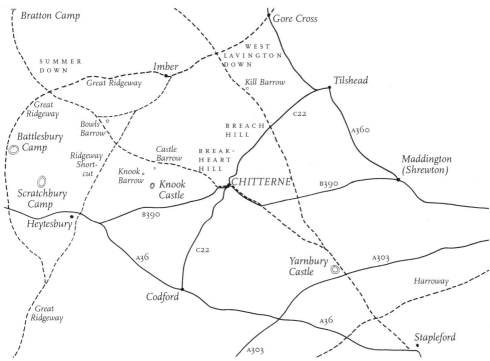

Ancient routeways around Chitterne. Modern roads are shown as solid lines for comparison.

As we have already seen Chitterne didn't occupy a high point on the chalk, nor did it occupy a prominent position on a major routeway, but two important connecting tracks passed through the village or nearby. These tracks connected the Great Ridgeway (Devon to the Wash) with the Harroway (Cornwall to Kent) and Old Sarum and Yarnbury Castle with Bratton Castle. They were much used to drive flocks of sheep to sheep fairs at Yarnbury and Bratton and by traders since the Bronze Age peddling their wares. Perhaps Edward of Salisbury travelled this route from his castle at Old Sarum when visiting his estates.

Many tracks converged at Old Sarum, the important seat of the Sheriff of Wiltshire, the same Edward. The particular track that interests us left Old Sarum and passed Stapleford on its way to Yarnbury Castle. Yarnbury is an old Iron Age enclosure that was still in use for sheep fairs in the early 20th century. Edith Olivier described travelling this road:

> 15 May 1935: To tea with Siegfried (Sassoon) driving via Yarnbro' (sic) Castle as when I have no car I shan't see these out of the way places but at this season the valleys excel the downs in beauty . . . [63]

At Yarnbury the track divided into two, one track passed through Chitterne and the other close by. First we'll look at the track that passed through the village, which eventually met the Great Ridgeway at Summerdown. This track, before it reaches Chitterne, crosses another old track from Codford to Maddington, in a dry valley that was also the boundary of Chitterne St Mary parish. Where the two tracks cross is a spot known as Oram's Grave.

We do not know Oram's first name, but he was a suicide buried near the parish boundary by the villagers, as was once the custom; with no funeral service, no written record, and a stake driven through the body. His story is known from the account told by a witness, and relayed via her neighbour to a local vicar. The witness, Elizabeth White, was returning home from Salisbury with her father when they came across the burial in progress. Her father told her, 'her maunt be vraughten at what she saw for they wouldn't hurt she',[64] and so she watched the man being buried. It is thought to have happened in 1805 or thereabouts. Oram was said to have hung himself due to disappointment in love.[65]

A little further on part of the track that passed through Chitterne became the Salisbury to Warminster coach road at the top of Shrewton Hill. It ran through the village for about a mile, first negotiating the very narrow and twisty Bidden Lane, which was straightened, raised and widened in the late 1960s. Then it merged with the C22 at The White Hart for a short distance as far as the Codford turning, crossed the brook, passed The King's Head and turned right at the Hollow and climbed the aptly named Breakheart Hill, eventually reaching Warminster via Sack Hill. This track over the downs continued to be the usual route from Salisbury to Warminster until the road through the Wylye Valley was constructed in the 18th century.[66]

The road from Heytesbury c.1910.

The Heytesbury Road or B390, formerly the A390, became the more usual route from Chitterne to Warminster after it was turnpiked in 1761. It is still the route to Warminster today. It is also the notoriously busy modern road, mentioned at the beginning of the chapter, which excites such debate amongst the villagers. Be that as it may, by the 18th century coach roads and turnpiked roads were well marked by milestones, too late for Samuel Pepys unfortunately. There is an old coach road milestone in the Hollow inscribed Sarum 14 Warminster 8.

A word here about the Amesbury Turnpike Trust that was set up following an Act of Parliament dated 1761, to deal with the poor state of the roads. The user of the road would in future pay by toll for its upkeep, rather than the landowner. The road ran from Amesbury to Heytesbury. Chitterne was on the Amesbury to Ansty Hill section.

The trust was headed by the Duke of Queensberry and the trustees included several Chitterne notables: Samuel Biggs, Christopher Michell, John Bulcher, Christopher Ingram and Francis Gibbs.[67] Messrs Samuel Biggs, Moody, Saunders

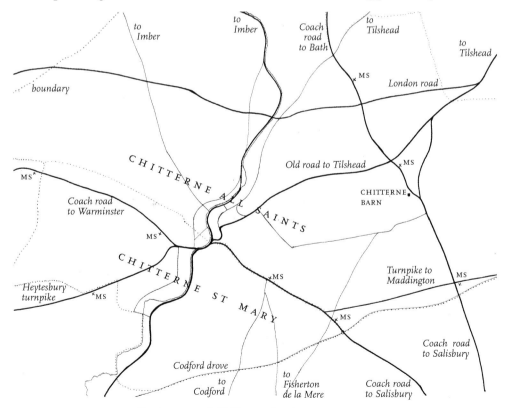

Routes around Chitterne about 200 years ago.

The junction of the road from Tilshead with the old Amesbury turnpike road. The two girls are standing where the Chitterne turnpike gates stood from 1761 to 1871. The toll booth was alongside Elm Farm on the left.

and Tinker of Chitterne between them advanced the sum of £870 towards the cost of setting up the Trust. In one year, 1780, £168.19s.0d. profit was made after salaries and repairs to the roads had been deducted.[68]

Tolls were collected in Chitterne at a tollbooth thought to have been in the grounds of Elm Farm. Widow Compton lived 'at ye gate' in 1784.[69] The turnpike gates stood on the old boundary between the two parishes of Chitterne All Saints and Chitterne St Mary, where the B390 meets the C22 from Tilshead. The road would have been much narrower in the 18th century. The barrier extended across the width of the Chitterne Brook, as well as the road, to catch those travellers who might try to avoid paying the toll by going through the water.

The Trust survived for just over 100 years, but by 1823 Chitterne's tolls were amalgamated with those of Heytesbury and by 1825 with Amesbury too. In 1871 the Trust was disbanded and the effects sold off.

To return to our tracks from Yarnbury. The second track that diverged at Yarnbury Castle headed northwest and passed close by Chitterne Barn (now removed). It joined the Chitterne to Tilshead road briefly at the top of Breach Hill, where the road kinks, and continued across country through the Imber Range to meet the Great Ridgeway at West Lavington Down. Part of this is the old Salisbury to Bath coach road, probably the one travelled by Samuel Pepys when he became lost.[70]

The old London Road passes close by Middle Barn Cottages, joins the current Chitterne to Tilshead road for a few hundred yards, again where the road kinks at the bottom of Breach Hill, and continues in a westerly direction across Breakheart Bottom. Its route is now lost as it enters the Imber range. These old roads across the downs were notorious haunts for highwaymen. Tales of treachery and robbery on the Plain are legendary and some connected with Chitterne have been recorded elsewhere but as no history of the village would be complete without them I will tell of them here. I know of three such tales and all involve victims returning home from market.

Robbers

Ella Noyes: 'There is always mystery on the Plain.'

William Lawne was killed on his way home to Maddington via Chitterne, from Warminster Market in 1666; his death is recorded in Maddington Church register. He was travelling with a large sum of gold and was followed and shot by the ostler from the inn where he had stayed. The killer took off with the money, but was captured and subsequently hung in chains just outside Maddington at the spot where the road from Tilshead and the road from Chitterne meet, as a reminder for all who might pass by.

Two robbers, Grimes and Baldwin, robbed several people returning from the market at Warminster before they were chased and shot, both on the same day in 1716. Grimes was shot by Edward Slade of Chitterne near Warminster Furze and brought dead to Imber and buried there the next day. Baldwin was shot by Dyke of Knook on West Lavington Sheep Down and taken alive to West Lavington, but soon died and was buried there. Grimes was an old offender but Baldwin stated before he died that it was his first offence. Edward Slade was a farmer from Chitterne, like others of his class, taking matters into his own hands in the absence

A stone monument erected on Chapperton Down, Chitterne at the spot where Benjamin Colclough died after attempting to rob Matthew Dean.

The inscription on the Chitterne Robber's Stone.

of any organised police force. Similarly the offenders in the next tale were chased and caught by farmers too.

Perhaps the most famous of these tales is that commemorated by a stone monument on Chapperton Down, Chitterne. It concerns the robbery of a farmer from Imber, called Dean, who was returning home from Devizes Market in 1839. Four men attempted to rob farmer Dean on the Lavington Road. They were chased, one of them, Benjamin Colclough, for 3 miles before dropping down dead on the spot marked by the stone near Chitterne. Colclough was buried in Chitterne without funeral rites. The other three, Thomas Saunders, George Waters and Richard Harris, were caught and transported to Australia for terms of 15 years. A second stone monument marks the spot where the robbery took place. Both monuments have metal plates inscribed with descriptions of the story as a warning to those passing by. This robbery was the last of its kind in the area. The establishment of banks in the market towns soon put paid to the highwaymen's trade, aided by the advent of the Wiltshire Constabulary no doubt.

Lost on the Plain

Besides the important tracks I have mentioned there are many less important tracks from Chitterne that head towards Codford, Fisherton Delamere, Imber, Tilshead and Shrewton. These lesser tracks were once marked by small piles of white chalkstones positioned at regular intervals alongside them. Village lore is full of narrow escapes and tragedies in the area, for the character of the Plain can change in a moment when darkness falls or the weather turns foul.

Frank Maidment, Baptist preacher at Chitterne from 1881-1952, recalled two times he was grateful for the chalk markers in the blackness of night up on the downs when returning from preaching at Imber's small Baptist Chapel. On the first occasion he was walking back to Chitterne in ever denser mist when, despite the guiding piles of chalk, he became lost. So he walked in progressively widening circles until he found a chalk pile and was able to resume his journey, only to find that in the confusion he was walking in the wrong direction, back towards Imber.

The second time he was returning to Chitterne with his pony and trap and in the dark he wandered from the track. For some time he walked about in the dark searching for the chalk heaps which would show his way again. In the meantime the pony had gone off to grass, but Mr Maidment had left one lamp burning on the trap so that he could find it again in the dark. He took the other lamp with him, found the track, and marked it with the lamp he was carrying. Then, stumbling across the downs without the aid of a light, he made for the lamp left burning on the trap. Afterwards, the lamp he had left on the track guided him towards it, although he confessed that he wasn't at all sure if he was heading for Chitterne or back to Imber. But eventually he got home all right.[71]

Another man of the cloth, the Rev. H.G. Rogers who was vicar of Chitterne 1895-1900, was caught out in the dark on the downs after visiting a parishioner and wandered lost for several hours. He was lucky; he was found by church members searching with lanterns and was none the worse for his ordeal. But poor little Norman Ashley, the four-year-old son of a shepherd, suffered a horrible fate in 1915. He was with his father, Frank Ashley, on the downs when a storm started so he set off for home, not too far distant. However, he got lost and was searched for all night by men with lamps, but he was not discovered until 11 o'clock the following morning. He was almost dead when he was found on Imber Down, about 3 miles from his home at Breach Hill Cottage, and there was no chance of saving his life.

Many times the prospect of shelter and a welcome in the village between the folds of downland has been a relief, not to say a lifesaver, for strangers to Chitterne. Whether a pilgrim seeking respite in the houses of the nuns of Lacock, in the 13th –14th centuries, or Samuel Pepys staying the night at The White Hart Inn when lost in 1668; or even a stranded car driver, unable to find a phone signal to call the AA in the 21st century; all were glad to find refuge here.

Samuel Pepys is the most famous person in history to take refuge in Chitterne. On 11 June 1668, at 6 o'clock in the evening he and his companions set out from Salisbury with a guide to pay a visit to Bath. Somewhere along their way they took a wrong turn and as darkness fell found themselves in Chitterne, legend has it at The White Hart Inn. The landlord cleared an already occupied room to accommodate his illustrious visitor, who declared in his diary that they found the: 'beds good, but lousy; which made us merry.' The next day they took the landlord with them as guide and arrived in Bath without problem before dark.

Until relatively recently Chitterne was a place to stop overnight or to change horses or to break a longer journey. How times change, nowadays a traveller would find no bed for hire in the village, no taxi and nowhere to get a car repaired. There have been carriers, motor coach and garage businesses at Chitterne in the past but they will be covered in a later chapter. For many years there was only one bus a week scheduled to take villagers to the nearest town, Warminster, and back. In 2007 there are bus services every day to Warminster, to Bath twice a week and to Devizes once a week. School children are transported to school in Warminster and Codford by bus or to Tilshead in private cars, the school mini-bus, or in taxis. Since writing this, the owners of St. Mary's Lodge have started a Bed and Breakfast business – a welcome addition to village facilities.

Paths

Village paths have wonderful local names such as: Baggerbush Path, Tyning, Long Hedge Path Mead and Craw Path. Some of these are old farm tracks, no longer used for their original purpose, but now well used by walkers who wish to explore the uncultivated downs beyond the fields of crops and pasture. In more recent times a new circuit of the live firing ranges, the Imber Range Perimeter Path (IRPP), has been waymarked. The IRPP passes through the village and is very popular with serious walkers, who may partake of welcome refreshment at The King's Head.

Walking about the village in the dark can be almost as hazardous as on the Plain, village residents are accustomed to arming themselves with a good torch, as, even in the 21st century we have no street lighting. A correspondent to the local paper said as long ago as 1902:

> We notice that a lamp is placed outside Mr Allsop's residence, which is a great boon to those whose business takes them out of doors these dark nights. The cost of this can only be trifling, and if the example was followed by others in Chitterne life would be worth living. It is not often that we have to thank the District Council for improvements in this village. It should be recorded therefore, that they have erected two posts in the middle of the footpath outside Mr Allsop's residence, which it is impossible to see on dark nights, and they are simply, therefore, a trap for unwary pedestrians to bump into. [72]

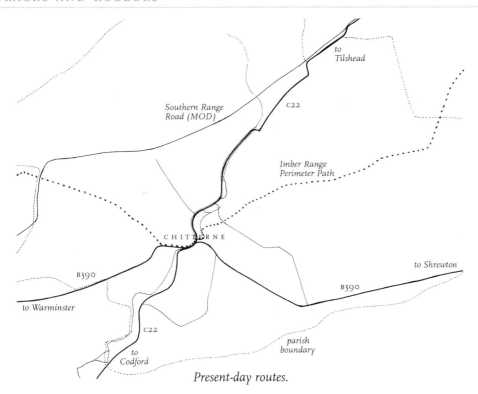

Present-day routes.

Besides the busy B390 Heytesbury to Shrewton Road already mentioned, another more minor road currently passes through Chitterne, it is the C22, a short road from Tilshead to Codford that intersects with the old Salisbury to Warminster coach road near the village green and the Church. The two roads join for 100 yards or so and then go their separate ways.

The C22 minor road faithfully follows the course of the Chitterne Brook through the village, indeed the bed of the brook most probably was the thoroughfare used by the inhabitants here in ancient times during the summer months. In the winter, when the brook filled, they would have used the two flanking paths on the banks of the stream, one of which is now the road. And in times of flood, two paths on higher ground that can be clearly seen on 19th century maps of the village, and still partially exist in Back Lane and Back Road.

The Winterbourne

The bed of the brook would have been much shallower in past times. It has been adapted and deepened over the centuries to suit the needs of the residents who

An area called Padham's Pool on an old map, where the road to Tilshead makes a sharp right turn near Middle Barn.

made their homes alongside this fickle stream. To see how the Chitterne Brook might have looked in ancient times take a look beyond the village outskirts, towards Tilshead, where the road makes a sharp right turn near Middle Barn Cottages. Straight ahead, beyond the bend is a low-lying area known as Padham's Pool, where the water spreads shallowly over the land in the wet season. Here you can imagine folk following the bed of the stream to get to Imber.

At the other end of the village alongside the road to Codford, the brook once divided into several smaller tributaries when this was an area of water meadows in the 18th century. Now it follows a course through the middle of a small field, formerly known as the 'Tithing field', opposite The King's Head.

The Tithing Field.

Within the village, bridges were constructed across the brook in several places. Clump Farm Bridge near the entrance to St Mary's Close and the footpath bridge opposite The Grange are two of the oldest. More have been added as they became necessary and the old hump-backed bridges at Townsend, previously known as the Arch, and Compton's Bridge near The King's Head have long since been flattened to suit the demands of military traffic. The latter was rebuilt again in 2004. At times of heavy rain and flood, water from both sides of the road to Warminster and one side of the road to Shrewton flowed into the brook. Small hump-backed bridges were built to allow residents dry access to their homes alongside these roads. Some of the roadside gullies were 3ft deep (1m).

Compton's Bridge. The old hump-backed bridge over the Chitterne Brook near Bridge Cottage.

The volume of water in the village varies considerably from year to year. Anything from flood in winter to dry wells in summer is possible. At Chitterne, chalk filtered water collects in a huge underground lake, held by a layer of impervious rock deep beneath the village. Come the winter rains, as the water table rises, so this water rises to the surface, bubbling and gurgling up as springs in gardens, through cracks in paving and concrete and even inside houses if they happen to be in the way; filling the wells, the brook, the drains and the meadows with some of the purest water available naturally anywhere. There were serious floods in the village in 1903, 1904, 1915 and 1925, and yet in 1900 only one well had any water, and in 1902 the wells were so dry that villagers had to rely on a cart to bring water from Codford every day. A villager recalls his grandfather transporting a Shrewton schoolteacher around the 1915 flood on the pillion of his motor-bike from the bottom of Heytesbury Road hill to the Shrewton Road[73].

Flood 1910.

One thing that rarely varies is the quality of the water. Water that has been filtered through chalk is noted for its purity. Until the 1960s, when mains water was brought to the village, most household-ers used well water but a few were fed from piped farm supplies. In 1965 six Chitterne households still hand-pumped their water[74]. Glebe Farm Cottages (Dolphin House), Sunnydene and the Round House used Glebe Farm water until 1992, when the regulations governing health and hygiene could no longer be met. The wells that still exist in the village are usually 50 or 60 feet deep (15 or 18m).

Flood 1925.

Although this natural phenomenon was a gift to the early settlers, by the 20th century something needed to be done to contain the abundance of water at times of flood. In the 1940s, Italian prisoners of war excavated the bed and banks of the stream and lined the bank nearest the roadside with concrete. Most years this remedy works, just occa-sionally nature has her way and the 'Cut' overflows again.

A Village Tour

In 1965 there were 256 villagers and 99 houses, 42 of which were owner-occupied. 83 houses had indoor sanitation.[75]

F OR THE PURPOSES of this chapter I am assuming Chitterne is one parish as it is today. I have explained its origins as two and possibly three parishes in an earlier chapter. Now, in 2007, around 300 villagers inhabit about 140 dwellings that together make the village a pleasant mix of the old and the new. A good proportion of the houses are large, a mix of flint chequered or banded stone, weathered red brick or rendered. These give the place an air of prosperity and history. Interspersed with newer houses in small closes are more reminders of the old days; rows of little cottages that originally sheltered farm workers and their families, and tile-topped old cob walls that once were thatched.

The village population is gently rising again. In 1965 there were 256 villagers as against the 298 in 2001,[76] and 40 years ago there were only 99 houses,[77] now I believe there are 139. This has happened despite a recent trend to convert two or more small cottages into one dwelling, usually to house a lot fewer people than lived in the space originally, which is thought provoking. As a result there has been an increase in the number of larger houses and less small ones available, especially for rent, but overall, new builds and conversions have cancelled out that reduction. Long gone are the days of little thatched cottages bursting with large farming families. It all goes to show just how much more prosperous we, the residents of Chitterne, are today and how much more space we need.

As the houses in Chitterne are numbered from the Tilshead end of the village, I shall start my tour there, at number 1, Townsend. But first a word or two of explanation concerning the names and arrangement of the village roads.

The main street through the village runs from the Tilshead end to the Heytesbury end and does not have a name, except for the first section, which is called **Townsend**. Possibly named after the landlord who once owned one or more properties, this section has been signed recently but with some controversy, as some villagers believe that Townsend ends at number 25, whereas the new sign has been positioned facing Brook Cottage, much further into the village. Some research is needed here to settle the dispute. However, the village houses are numbered consecutively starting from number 1 at the Tilshead end to number 109 at the Heytesbury end, with detours up the left side and down the right side of unsigned **Bidden Lane**, and along the unsigned **Codford Road** on the way. The censuses tend to call this main village street: 'High Street', but that is not its name and the locals call the section from Bridge Cottage to the Round House just 'Street'. **Bidden Lane** is the correct name for the road that extends from Elm Farm up the hill towards Shrewton, (sometimes spelt Bitten Lane on the censuses), but nowadays it is often referred to as **Shrewton Road**, and to the locals it is known as 'The Lane.' It was a narrow, twisty and insignificant road until the late 1960s, when the surface was raised, straightened and widened, and the junction at Elm Farm was altered to its present appearance. **Back Road** originally extended in a loop from Elm Farm (near the Green), around the back of the

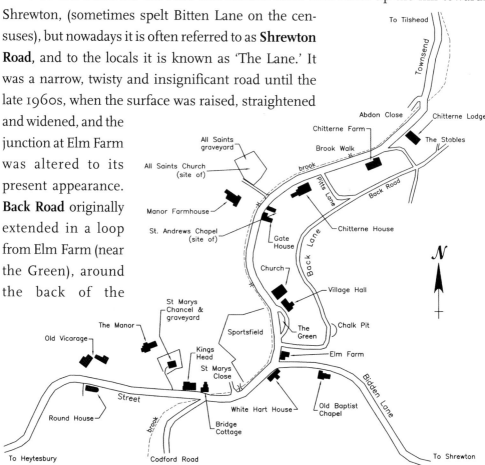

- 50 -

church to rejoin the village road between Chitterne Lodge and Chitterne Farm. But the first section from Elm Farm to Pitt's Lane was changed a few years back, at the request of the residents, to **Back Lane. Pitt's Lane** is a short lane joining Back Road to the main village street. **Abdon Close**, off Townsend, was so named after prominent village resident Abdon Polden. **St Mary's Close**, created in the mid 1970s from the site of Clump Farm's pig unit, leads off the village street near the sportsfield.

The Village Tour

Abdon Polden the stonemason built number 1 Townsend on a piece of land that he owned and named it **Alma Cottage** after his eldest daughter. He and his wife Jane lived there with their eight children in 1881.[78] Another field he owned became the site of the first Council-built houses in Chitterne, hence the name **Abdon Close**. Abdon's daughter, Florence, and her husband Alfred Burt, lived at Alma Cottage with Abdon until his death in 1924 and for the rest of their own lives. Alfred Burt was a blacksmith and prominent member of the community. He was captain of the bell-tower at church, trainer of the village tug-o-war team, parish councillor

Alma Cottage with Alf Burt in his Special Constable's uniform.

and Father Christmas for the children's Christmas party. He died in 1957 and Florence in 1968. Another resident of number 1 was Peter Goodwright, the impersonator, and his wife Norma who was lay reader at the church. The Goodwrights also joined in many village events. They renamed the cottage **Dru-Wry** and lived here for several years during the late 20th century.

A century ago Townsend was made up of thatched farmworkers' cottages for the most part. Today there is no thatch and many cottages have been demolished and not all of them replaced. The contrast between the Townsend cottages and their nearest neighbour would be even more striking if this impressive stone and flint house faced the street, but it merely presents its rear towards the row of cottages with a disdainful air. **Chitterne Lodge** is one of Chitterne's listed buildings and has

Townsend. The thatched cottages in the foreground have been replaced by modern buildings.

served as a farmhouse, a guest house and the home of a racehorse trainer during the 300 plus years of its existence. It was built in the late 17th century and extended in the 18th and 19th centuries. It originally formed part of the estate belonging to the Lord of the Manor until the end of the Longs ownership early in the 20th century. Then in 1905 the Chitterne Lodge Estate, comprising Chitterne Lodge and

Chitterne Lodge.

Chitterne Farm was renovated and offered for sale. It was sold to Ronald Farquharson[79] who also bought a 412-acre property next door called Wroughton's, which became the site of **Chitterne Stables**. The War Department, now the Ministry of Defence, compulsorily purchased the whole estate after Farquharson's death. During World War II the Lodge was used to house soldiers. After the war the MoD continued as landlord to a succession of horse trainers. One of their tenants was Jim Ford.[80] Jim's wife Mary ran Chitterne Lodge as a guest house, even after Jim's early death, when a new trainer, Ian Dudgeon, arrived in the village to take over the stables. It was he who had **Paddock House** built for himself, alongside Chitterne Lodge; thus Chitterne Lodge and the stables parted company. Chitterne Lodge is now privately owned and **The Stables** have been converted into a courtyarded group of eight cottages.

Chitterne Farmhouse.

Chitterne Farmhouse and its associated farmworkers cottages: the listed Victorian **Flint Cottage** next door, and the 1950s **Chitterne Farm Cottages** formed part of the Chitterne Lodge estate. The farmhouse was enlarged in 1881[81], when Walter Long owned the estate. Joseph and Louisa Dean, farmers from Imber, were the first tenants, having moved from The Lodge.[82] For a long time I assumed this referred to Chitterne Lodge, but recently an 1896 sale document has caused me to think

again. This document names a house that we know today as **The Grange**, as 'The
Lodge.' There can be no mistaking the building in question, for the description fits
The Grange Estate, as it was then, perfectly, including the farm buildings that later
became **Long House**. Further checks have shown that Chitterne Lodge and The
Lodge both existed at the same time in Chitterne All Saints parish, so I am sure that
the Deans lived in The Lodge, before moving into the newly enlarged Chitterne
Farmhouse. Question: Who changed the name of the Lodge to The Grange and
when? More details about Chitterne Farm will be found in the Farming chapter.

Opposite the farmhouse is number 29, **Robin's Rest**, a cottage formerly owned
by the MoD. A pair of semi-detached thatched cottages once stood alongside Robin's Rest, opposite Flint House, on the northern bank of the Chitterne Brook. They
were demolished many years ago and replaced by a more modern row of four
farmworkers' houses, set back further from the road, known as numbers 1 to 4
Brook Walk. These were built to house the workers of Manor Farm and they were
originally approached by a footpath bridge over the brook, as were all dwellings on
the north side of the brook. Some footbridges have been replaced in latter years by
wider structures that allow access by vehicles.

Flint House was home to Clement Polden, who was one half of Polden and
Feltham, carpenters and wheelwrights. The house stood in Polden and Feltham's
yard facing away from the street. After Clements's death, his sons Owen and Alban

*The Tilshead road. Flint House on the left, and beyond Robin's Rest on the right are the cottages
that have been demolished.*

lived in Flint House with their widowed mother and ran the business. Owen made a shop window facing the street to display lawn mowers and gardening accessories in the later days. Alban Polden, married his cousin, Olive Burt, and built the first bungalow in the village, **The Walnut Tree**, in the garden of Flint House, facing Back Lane/Road. Owen Polden sold up in 1972 and later the shop was demolished and a new wing added to the house. The sheds at the side of Flint house, which once housed the smithy, carpenter's shop and paint and plumbing shop, still exist, but the deep sawing pit has long been filled in.[83]

    Pitt's House, number 31, also has historical business associations. This 'L' shaped brick and flint building was once a row of farmworker's cottages. Walter Hume Long had it built in 1891, probably to replace an earlier building. In 1925 it housed five families, one of these, Charles and Eliza Mundy's family, had nine children and another, Frank and Helen Sheppard's had six. Frank Sheppard and family lived in the part facing the street, where Frank ran his repair business, which is covered in another chapter.

William and Harriet (née Polden) Windsor with their sons Keith and Cecil at Pitt's Cottage in 1895.

    Richard Hayward, the then owner of the Chitterne House estate, built **Pitt's Cottage**, number 34, behind Pitt's House at the end of Pitt's Lane, in 1870. It bears a plaque to this effect at the front. It was probably built to house the Chitterne House gardener; the grandparents of Bill Windsor lived there for many years. In 1925 gardener Sidney Bacon and his wife Ada were the occupants.

    Hiding behind a brick wall topped with pleached limes is **Chitterne House**, another of the village's listed houses. It is part of a small estate that includes The Gate House and a much newer housekeeper's cottage. Chitterne House was built c1680 by the Michell family and added to 100 years later. Robert Michell lived there in 1773[84]. A portion of the house facing the road is of banded stone and flint, with mullioned windows. An additional section behind is built of brick; both wings have slated roofs. There is a datestone over the door with an inscription: 'Health and peace this house increase 1635', which has possibly been moved from an earlier position[85]. The house was bought from the Michells in 1830 by Richard Hayward senior of Beechingstoke, and passed down to his son, Richard Hayward junior, an eccentric, who died childless in 1913. Admiral Charles Napier was owner from 1913, and then Lady Dugdale, lady-in-waiting to Queen Mary. The village children turned out to cheer Queen Mary when she paid a visit to Lady Dugdale in 1928, but embarrassment ensued when the royal car was too wide to pass through the Chitterne House gates, and the Queen was forced to alight in the road and walk in. Hugely mortified, Lady Dugdale had the gateway widened, but the Queen never paid a return visit. Part of the staircase in the main entrance hall is said to have been brought from Heale House, in the Woodford valley, home of a family related to Lady Dugdale. Lt.Col. Peter Sykes bought the estate from Lady Dugdale in 1947[86] and it remains in the family today.

   The Gate House, an associated outbuilding, arched gateway and wall, all listed, is one of the oldest buildings in the village, probably only St Mary's Chancel is older. The site that it occupies is very ancient and probably dates back to at least Saxon times. The present buildings date from the 1500s and were probably either rebuilt after being struck by lightening during a terrible thunderstorm in 1447, or constructed by the new owners after the dissolution of Lacock Abbey. The original

The Gate House painted by John Buckler c.1805.

The back of the Gate House painted by John Buckler c.1805.

building is said, according to local legend, to have been built as a hospice for pilgrims or travellers on their way to Lacock. But it appears later to have been used as a farmhouse; a base for the nuns' sheep farm in Chitterne. The Morgan family were the main tenants of the nuns of Lacock and still lived here in 1539 at the dissolution.[87] After the dissolution The Gate House was acquired by Thomas Temys, brother of the last Abbess of Lacock, and the lease passed through marriage to William Jordan. In his will of 1602 William Jordan left his wife the leases of two farms previously held by Lacock Abbey, a sheep farm and a land farm.[88] One of them must have been based at The Gate House. He lived the other side of the road in Manor Farm and Manor Farm and The Gate House have long been connected, as we shall see. 12th century St Andrew's Chapel, which was held by Bradenstoke Priory before the dissolution, is thought to have stood behind the outbuilding that is now used as a garage; several stone coffins were unearthed on the spot.[89] Later in the 17th century the Michells acquired the buildings and the line of ownership is the same as for Chitterne House. The Gate House was used as a farmhouse from the early days until 1975, when it was refurbished for Lt Col Sykes' widow.[90] It has been much altered during its long existence; an early 19th century painting of it by John Buckler shows an extra wing at the back that no longer exists. There are many legends concerning this site; a cross carved in the roadside wall of the building marks the spot where 10 year-old Jane Grant was crushed to death by a traction engine in 1905. Her brother Freddie is said to have marked the exact spot with Jane's spilt blood at the time and later carved the memorial cross permanently into one of the blocks of limestone with his penknife. Another legend concerns a tunnel that is supposed to exist between The Gate House and Manor Farm opposite. It has been said that in the days of horses and carts, you could hear them rattling over the hollow tunnel beneath the road[91].

The remains of the old Manor Farmhouse after the fire in 1852 painted by W.W. Wheatley.

The original **Manor Farmhouse**, like The Gate House, was a very ancient building and certainly once part of the estate owned by the Earls of Salisbury and given by them before 1184 to the Priory of Bradenstoke, near Lyneham. In 1824 Hoare described it thus: 'another good house, having on its front the following shield: A chevron between three lozenges, on a chief three martlets. This coat belongs to one branch of the family of Jordan.' The family he refers to is the same William Jordan mentioned earlier, who acquired the manor of All Saints in 1580 from his wife's brother John Temys,[92] who was a nephew of Joan Temys, the last Abbess of Lacock. The manor remained in the Jordan family for about 80 years, passed to the Giles family of Fisherton Delamere, then to John Holder who sold it to Paul Methuen in 1771. Methuen's son offered it for sale in 1815 and the Onslow-Michell family acquired it. In 1852 Manor Farmhouse was burnt beyond repair in a disastrous fire. It seems that the fire started about noon on a Saturday in mid April in the large farmyard, which was thickly covered with 'muckle'. The weather had been dry and so the flames soon took hold over the entire area, enveloping the yard pump and spreading quickly to the surrounding farm buildings and then to the house, where the tenant farmer, Harry Hitchcock, lay in his sickbed. He was swiftly moved to the safety of a neighbouring house owned by a Mr Hayward, which must be Chitterne House or The Gate House. Both Heytesbury and Warminster fire engines attended but were unable to prevent the destruction of three wheat ricks, a barley mow, six calves, twelve pigs, eighteen head of poultry and machinery and implements of considerable value, besides all the farm buildings.[93] The Hitchcock family were tenants of Sir Henry Onslow and are known to have farmed at All Saints Manor Farm for many years, as the number of Hitchcock graves in All Saints graveyard testify. They were no strangers to tragedy as the burials include four of family members who died under twenty-five years of age. The fire was probably the last straw. Harry Hitchcock died later that year and by 1900 there were no Hitchcocks in Chitterne at all.

Manor Farmhouse in 1984.

The present Manor Farmhouse was built after 1852, of banded limestone and flint, with a tiled roof and stone chimneystacks. After passing from the Onslows to the Collins family, who lived in and farmed Manor Farm themselves it was acquired by the War Dept before World War II and reverted to a tenancy. The house, stables and paddock were sold to a private buyer in 1984. See the Farming chapter for more on Manor Farm.

Manor Farm had seven tied cottages at the time of the 1815 sale; **Brook Cottage** was one. A pretty, late 18th century chequered flint and limestone listed building, lying beyond the brook, near the new entrance to Manor Farm. The rest of the Manor Farm tied cottages are obscured by time, but probably included the now demolished thatched cottages numbers 27 and 28. Later the Mansion House stables (now Coach House) were converted into farmworkers cottages for Manor Farm and, as already mentioned, the Brook Walk terrace was built too.

Old **All Saints Vicarage** stood on a plot of land between All Saints churchyard and the road, it was removed when the two parishes were combined under one vicar and the material used to repair and enlarge the vicarage in Chitterne St Mary. The plot of land on which it stood was exchanged with Mr Walter Long for the plot that he owned next to the new vicarage, which became the vicarage tennis ground. Mr Long afterwards gave his new plot to Sir William Onslow, owner of Manor Farm, on condition that he should give a piece of land for the enlargement of the All Saints graveyard.

Perhaps it would be as well to complete the Manor estate here by including the **Mansion House** itself. I am calling it that for want of a correct name, it has also been known locally as **The Great House.** The name **Milbourne's Court** occurs in 17th century records of the village, but location unknown, so it is possible that the Mansion House and Milbourne's Court were one and the same. Besides the lack of a definite name, there is to date no description of the house that once stood in the present day sportsfield behind the remains of the listed flint and limestone chequered wall. But it was part of the estate of the Earls of Salisbury, and thus, with its associated stables, came to be held by Lacock Abbey. If the Mansion House was Milbourne's Court then after the dissolution it was held by Matthew Ley and later Sir John Danvers who forfeited the house by Act of Parliament in 1661, for his part in the regicide of King Charles the first in 1649. Paul Methuen sold the Mansion House to Matthew Michell in 1775/6.[94] It was demolished in the early 1820s and the site, known as Whitsuntide Field and home of the annual Whitsuntide Fete,[95] belonged to the Collins family, then the War Department, who sold it to the village in the 1950s, since when it has been used as the village sportsfield. The stables were converted to farmworker's cottages,[96] known locally as **Great Houses** or **Big**

Houses, and to a single private dwelling in the 20th century, known as **Coach House**. It is a listed building of banded flint and limestone. Perhaps the Mansion House was of similar appearance.

Backtracking a little to **The Grange**, a listed early 19th century farmhouse of stucco with a Welsh slate roof and brick chimneystacks, which I mentioned earlier was known as **The Lodge** when put up for sale in 1896 by Walter Long. At that time it had outbuildings, lawns, gardens and a paddock and William Beak was the farmer. The main outbuilding comprised two coach houses, stabling for three horses, a harness room, boot house, housekeeper's room and servants' hall downstairs, with six servants' rooms and a hay and corn loft above, all later converted to one house. The two houses together became known as **Holmrooke Grange**. They were owned and let by Col. Morse at the end of World War 1. After World War 2 Group Captain Leo Maxton and his wife owned the estate, including a paddock behind the village school, which they often allowed the school to use, and another behind **Yew Tree Cottage**, which they sold to Archie Dean for £1000. [97] In the 1970s the little estate was split and the two houses were sold separately, they became The Grange and **Long House**. Alan Fair and his wife owned the Grange, and Captain Paddy O'Riordan RN and his family Long House. In 2003 Long House was renamed **Holmrooke House**.

The Grange c.1920.

Chitterne Church and the old school are covered in another chapter.

The new **Village Hall**, on the site occupied by the previous hall, originally the village school, was opened on the 13th February 1999. After two open village meetings it was decided to spend any funds raised on a new hall rather than the old one, which was in need of many repairs. The new building was designed by George Batterham of Batterham Matthews Designs, Marshfield, Chippenham. It has two interconnecting halls that can be used independently or together. The overall effect is one of simplicity and space. Natural wood has been used to good effect, including the re-use of the old beams from the former hall. The original estimate of the cost was £91,000, but the final bill came to £160,000, the monies having been raised by grants, fundraising and donations.

The Village Hall.

Three homes face the green: number 43/44, **Yew Tree Cottage** or **Bow House** as it now is; numbers 45 and 46, **Woodbine Cottages**, now **Woodbine Cottage** and **The Poplars**. Archie Dean, of Yew Tree Cottage, who bought the paddock, also replaced the cottage thatch with tiles and built the large sheds behind; he was the father of Graham Dean who ran Bridge Garage for many years. Before Archie's time the building was two dwellings; Frank Polden lived there in the 1920s, the Le Cocq family from the Channel Islands in wartime, and in the late 1950s/early 60s William and Emily Coates; the King family in the 1970s, and later the homeopath Henrietta Wells. Woodbine Cottages once housed the county police; the county paid £332.9s.2d. for it in 1906. Previously the village policemen had lodged in

Elm Farm.

various houses in the village. Len Champion was the last village policeman to live
in Chitterne. The Poplars was the home of another family of Poldens for many
years; it was also the village smithy and has in its garden the remains of the Penny
Reading Room. Arthur Polden, son of Abdon, and his wife Louisa lived there from
the 1920s to 1950. Arthur was one of the Polden Brothers building firm, he died in
1935, and after Louisa's death in 1950 their son Ernest Polden, and his wife Dorothy,
lived in the house until 1979.[98] **The Penny Reading Room** in Back Lane behind the
Poplars was once thatched. It was briefly licensed for weddings when the new church
was being built in 1861 and was still being supported by fund-raising activities in
1901.[99] Next-door are two new houses. A self-build house, **Kirrin House**, originally
called **Navarac** (caravan in reverse), after the temporary home the builders lived in
on site during construction, and **Peppercorn House**.

    Elm Farm is a listed early 19th century stuccoed house with a tiled roof and a
fine cast roof ridge. It was the childhood home of John Wallis Titt, the engineer,
from 1841 until his early twenties.[100] The house has been divorced from its farmland and farmyard for many years, since coming under the ownership of the WD.
The farmyard and barns were used as a depot by the Defence Properties Service
Agency until a few years ago. Now the barns have gone and the site contains two
new houses: **Buttercups** and **Hawthorn Cottage**, and, on an old orchard beyond the

The top of Bidden Lane c.1940. The cottages on the right were later demolished.

yard, are two more houses, numbers 1 and 2 **Apple Orchard.** Around the corner past the drive to Syringa Cottage, is the old chalk pit.[101] Tony Newton, son of Maurice Newton of The White Hart, once owned this. He gained permission to build there about 30 years ago, but his plan was never completed. The footings of the proposed building are still visible.

The **Chitterne Tollbooth** for the Amesbury Turnpike Trust is thought to have been in the grounds of Elm Farm 1761-1871; George Jones was the gatekeeper in 1841.[102] Possibly the small brick shed-type building in the front garden on the corner of the road is all that remains of this structure since the road was widened in the 20th century.[103]

In Bidden Lane were rows of farmworkers' cottages; many still exist. Part of number 53, **Syringa Cottage,** is all that remains of one row. Chitterne's famous detective, Bill Brown of Scotland Yard, had Syringa Cottage built for his retirement in the 1930s; incorporated into it is the cottage where he was brought up. Most of the lost cottages on the Chitterne St Mary side of the lane, were demolished before the road was widened and raised in the 1960s. The old post office and shop, part of number 93, **Chapel Cottage**, had two steps before the road was raised to the height of the post office doorway (now a window). The bakehouse that once stood near the road between the shop and the chapel has gone and the **Baptist Chapel** is now a private dwelling.[104]

Number 94, **Well House**, or **Well Cottage** as it is now, is a listed late 18th century house, thought to have been the first home of the Wallis family in Chitterne. The infamous **Village Hut**, an ex-army World War 1 wooden hut used for social occasions between 1921 and 1970, once stood on what is now part of the garden. The handrail and steps can still be seen.

On the corner of Bidden Lane opposite Elm Farm stands **White Hart House**, formerly **The White Hart Inn**, famous locally for having accommodated Samuel Pepys for one night in 1668 when he became lost on Salisbury Plain on his way to Bath.[105] This listed building is one of the few in Chitterne that can be dated with some certainty; it has 1651 inscribed above the door and was constructed of coursed rubble and stone with a thatched, now clay-tiled, roof. A large shed, now converted to a garage, alongside the inn is a reminder of the days when a carrier business was run in tandem with the alehouse.[106] In 1896 there was a barn, stables, cowsheds and a one acre paddock,[107] part of this ground now holds a row of four new cottages: **Clockhouse Cottages.**

Local builders, Polden Brothers, built listed number 96 on a vacant holding known as Clear Springs. Named no doubt on account of the springs that bubbled out of the ground when the water table rose. It was home to Edward Polden's family and over the years he attempted to tame the springs. It has been renamed several times since; from 1916 to 1935 the Razey family called it **The Laurels**, and in Evelyn Feltham's time it was known simply by its number: 96. Pete and Liz Ash, 1976 to 2004, returned to its roots and renamed it **Clear Spring House**. Now it is called **Pear Tree House.**

Clump House, originally **Clump Farm** is a listed brick and tile house, with pretty headed fireplace surrounds inside, built early in the 19th century and named after the hill behind the farm. Paul Methuen was Lord of the Manor at the time and most probably had the house built. John Veal, yeoman farmer, was the first tenant with a 99-year lease in 1802;[108] the Stratton family of Codford were the last to own the farm, their tenants were the Garland family in 1937.[109] After the end of its days as a farmhouse the house was home to the Oliver family and it was they who had **Clump Cottage** built on part of the garden in 1986. Although the cottage is a smaller building, notice that its façade is a deliberate copy of the front of Clump House. The Clump Farm pig unit on the opposite side of the road to the house was sold for building in the 1970s and a close of seven detached houses erected on it, called **St Mary's Close**. The original bridge to the pig farm, **Clump Farm Bridge**, is a listed

Clump House.

example of an 18th century limestone and brick bridge.

The former Clump Farm cowsheds, once used for garaging, have recently been demolished at the **Old Malthouse**, next door to Clump Cottage. The listed Old Malthouse is older than Clump House, being 18th century; Paul Methuen leased it to Charles Baker in 1802 when John Veal was farming next door. It was in use as a malthouse until the Wallis family ceased malting their own barley after the punitive tax imposed in 1910. For a year, between 1903 and 1904, with the agreement of Farmer Wallis, it was home to the beer-shy Baptists after their chapel was destroyed by fire.[110] One wonders how they coped with the pervasive fumes of the malting process. It was later home to the dairyman at Clump Farm and known as **Pine Cottage** for the large Monkey Puzzle Tree in the front garden. The author and Times journalist Ferdinand Mount lived in the Old Malthouse at one time, as did Francis Gyngell and his doctor wife, Hester, who died in 1993.

The village numbering system has until now followed some sort of plan, but not so in Codford Road. The two old buildings there, **Meadow Cottage** and number **98**, are numbered in reverse order; for Meadow Cottage, which is number 99, precedes number 98. It makes no sense, however, I will stick with my plan and deal with house numbers consecutively. Number 98 is a listed building of early 19th century dressed limestone with a Welsh slate roof. It was the home of William James Feltham, one half of the Polden and Feltham business; it remains in the Feltham family to this day.

Returning to the main road. Opposite the end of Codford Road is 17th century listed **Bridge Cottage**, number 100, so named because it sits alongside a bridge over the Chitterne Brook. The bridge was once hump-backed and known locally as

Compton's Bridge, when generations of the Compton family occupied the Cottage, which Ann Compton purchased from Walter Long for £55 in 1896. She was the last of the family to live there.[111] Since the Comptons' time Bridge Cottage has had a varied career. Henry Slater and Lily Poolman ran 'Ye Olde Bridge Café' in the single storey annexe they added at the back; a café started up for servicemen in World War II. John Withers carried it on and ran a coach business and one petrol pump until the mid-1950s. From 1955 Linda Dean kept the café going for a few years and then concentrated on the bed and breakfast business and her husband Graham ran **Bridge Garage** from an outbuilding and served petrol from two pumps near the roadside. In 1971 the Deans moved to Deptford but kept Bridge Cottage and rented it out, until 1996 when they sold it to Ross Sharpe.[112] Graham and Linda's son and his wife built **Hengistbury Cottage** in 1991 at the rear of Bridge Garage. When Graham retired and closed Bridge Garage down, the garage building was added to the new cottage.[113]

The only public house in the village, **The King's Head**, is a listed mid 19th century building of flint and limestone with a formerly thatched, now tiled, roof. This inn was once called **The George Inn**; it burnt down under the tenure of Thomas Bennet, and was afterwards let to James Wheeler in 1742.[114] In 1896 there was a bar, bar parlour, sitting room, smoking room, tap room, kitchen, back kitchen and larder with four bedrooms over. An adjoining cottage, since incorporated into the main building, was being used as a store-room, but had once been a small shop. Outside, behind and at the side of the pub in 1896, were a brewhouse, stables for eleven horses, a large clubroom, (at one time a skittle alley), outhouses and a walled-in kitchen garden. At the front between the pub and the

The King's Head in the early 1900s.

road there was a weighbridge. The grounds in all totalled 2 roods 26 perches.[115] Since that time the pub lands have been carved up; in 1928 the then owners, Ushers Brewery, gave a portion to the Church for an extension to St Mary's graveyard and later owners, Gibbs Mew sold a plot for building number **101**. The kitchen garden, the stables and skittle alley are long gone; now replaced by a beer garden and a car park.[116]

Birch Cottage, a modern house, occupies the site of the former Chitterne Tithe Barn.[117] Behind it lies the chancel of the former Church of Chitterne St Mary; this is covered in another chapter.

The Manor, home to the Wallis family since 1851, is one of my favourite village buildings. Tudor most probably, although labelled 'mid 17th century' in Listed Buildings, and originally built in an 'H' plan, it has Tudor fireplaces and the original stairs, but no longer has the eastern wing. It is built of mellow red bricks on a limestone plinth, with limestone mullioned windows and a stone slate roof, and is sited, as befits a manor house, overlooking the parish. Even the old barns and stables remain, though they are not so old as the house. It was part of the Lord of the Manor's estate and early tenants include the Sanders family, farmers, who lived in Chitterne from the 17th century for almost 200 years and some of whom are remembered in the chancel, and Christopher Fricker, Solicitor and farmer. In 1851 William Wallis rented The Manor and 460 acres of land from Lord Long, who was lord of the manor at the time, Paul Methuen was lord before Walter Long. After World War 1 Frederick Wallis took up a mortgage to buy the Manor and 460 acres from Lord Long. The mortgage was not paid off until Frederick's son Victor's time. Legend has it that there is a tunnel running from the Manor's cellars, possibly to the Mansion House, now demolished, that once stood on the present day village sportsfield[118].

Opposite the Manor is **St Mary's Lodge**, formerly three cottages for the Manor farmworkers, numbered **101**, **102** and **103**. Len Searchfield, the plumber, and his mother-in-law Sarah Williams and families lived there in 1925. Two of the cottages were converted into one dwelling for the present Wallis family of the Manor when they married. Later all three were knocked together and Mr Scott-Bolton, who negotiated the purchase of the sportsfield from the MoD for the village, lived there until 1978.

Ivy Cottage, an old thatched cottage, once the home of Mark and Mary Poolman, was demolished to make way for a modern house, number **104**. Numbers 105 and

The Heytesbury road c.1940. Glebe Farmhouse on the right and from the left The Manor farm cottages, Ivy Cottage, Glebe Farm Cottages and the Round House.

106, **Glebe Farm Cottages**, were farmworkers' cottages for Glebe Farm. George Furnell lived in 105 and Mark Titt in 106 at the turn of the 20th century when they were known as **Vicarage Cottages**. There may once have been three cottages here because the two sections at either end of the terrace are of brick, and brick, flint and rubble, with slate roofs, but the middle section is rendered with a tiled roof, which was once thatched. They were converted into one house, **Dolphin House**, in 2000. The adjacent paddock contains the new **Glebe Farmhouse**. Constructed for the owners of Glebe Farm, the Lockyer family, some years ago, but since sold and enlarged.

The original Glebe Farmhouse is opposite Dolphin House and sited at right angles to the road. This c1650-1700 listed building, made of brick with stone quoins and a tiled roof, is now named **Glebe House**, numbers 107 and 108. The small single storey annexe nearest the road was once a separate dwelling. Before 1800 Thomas Sanders, son of James Sanders who farmed The Manor[119] occupied the farmhouse. It appears that for many years the two farms were closely associated, as members of the extended Wallis family of The Manor lived there too. For instance: when Victor Wallis farmed at The Manor his younger brother Donald farmed Glebe Farm. Donald's widow stayed on at the farmhouse after her husband's death but the farmland was sold, and that was when the farmhouse became separated from the farm.[120]

Number 109, or **The Round House**, which has also been known as **Laura Cottage** and **Tower House**, is my house. It is a listed house, the central section built c1680, the round end c1814 and the western end in 1986. The oldest parts are of rendered stone and flint, with brick window and doorway surrounds and a slate roof. A stable for three horses with a hayloft over is of rubble encased in brick, with a slate roof. Some believe the house was a tollhouse, as the listed buildings description suggests, but local legend has it as a seafarer's folly, and this is nearer the truth. The round end was added in the time of Charles Morris, who had been in the navy, and lived here for over 60 years until his death in 1879. Inside, the round rooms differ in character to the rest of the house; they are of Regency design, with higher ceilings, larger, shuttered sash windows as opposed to casements, and moulded architraves and skirtings. After Charles died, Walter Long the owner let the house to a series of tenants, before selling it in 1897 to Alice Langford, granddaughter of Farmer Wallis at The Manor. In 1917 George Poolman bought it and it passed to William and Elsie Poolman at George's death. In 1963 the half-acre garden was divided in two, and William's youngest son had a bungalow built on one half. He lives there still, at **Sunnydene**. The Round House remained in the Poolman family until 1976 when we bought it. [121]

Across the road is the imposing **Old Vicarage**, formerly St Mary's Vicarage. In 1812, when the Reverend John Batchellor was Vicar of Chitterne All Saints and Chitterne St Mary, £540 was borrowed from the Governors of the Bounty of Queen Anne by mortgaging the Glebe lands to fund this building. The new vicarage was sited on the edge of Chitterne St Mary, at the bottom of the hill facing the road from Heytesbury, in a position where it must have immediately become a landmark. It is still an imposing building today, with its grey slate roof, and pale-pink, washed walls setting off the distinctive regency canopy shading the ground floor windows facing the road. To the side and rear is a range of brick outbuildings. At the side of the house there is a stable for two horses, a tack room and a carriage house with a hayloft above, and tucked away behind the house, a rare example of a two-holer privy. In 1819 when the All Saints Vicarage was demolished, the material was used to repair and enlarge St Mary's Vicarage. Rev. William Swayne, vicar of Chitterne 1874 -1883, painted sketches in oils on the vicarage shutters and doors but they have since been obliterated. When Rev. Arthur Hawkes resigned as vicar in 1954, the Ecclesiastical Commissioners arranged for a firm from Salisbury to refurbish the neglected vicarage. Many beech trees, which had grown tall enough to hide the building from the road, were cut down. The Vicarage remained the home of the incumbent until the parishes of Chitterne and Tilshead were linked under one vicar in the 1960s, and a new vicarage was built in Tilshead. Since then, as **St Mary's House**, it passed through the hands of several different owners but, remarkably, the interior layout remained much the same as it must have been in Victorian or even Regency times. There are distinct 'front' and 'back of house' areas, recalling times when the Vicar and his family were waited on by serving staff, but nowadays the garden is much smaller and the stable has been used as a garage until recently.

When Dennis and Yvonne Nayler owned St Mary's House they had a bungalow built in the 1990s for Yvonne's elderly parents, on part of the garden adjoining Glebe House, and called it **Little St Mary's**. The Naylers had a new house built for themselves on another part of the garden next to the Hollow, probably the old tennis ground and before that the site of an old cottage, to which they transferred the name **St Mary's House**. Their old house was renamed: **Old Vicarage**. Recently the present owners of the Old Vicarage have refurbished the stable building and returned it to its original use.

There are a few outlying houses beyond the village numbering system. **Valley Farm** is a modern house, built in the last 20 years on land at the southwestern end of the village that was previously part of The Manor farm.[122] **Middle Barn**, numbers 1 and 2, alongside the road to Tilshead, are the last remaining examples of the many field barn cottages that were once scattered outposts around the village. These semi-detached houses were built in 1915, much later than most and have not impinged on the activities of the MoD, so they have survived the fate of the others. A red brick-built house, **New House Farm**, known locally as **Mason's**, stood at the top of Shrewton Hill, where a lone wooden shed remains. Maurice Gagen lived and farmed there at the end of World War 1, then the Rev Thomas and Lewis Downs Mason.[123] The last occupier before demolition in the 1980s was Jack Walberton who was employed at Chitterne Farm.[124]

Village People

The poetry of history lies in the quasi-miraculous fact that once, on this familiar spot of ground, walked other men and women, as actual as we are today, thinking their own thoughts, swayed by their own passion, but now all gone, one generation vanishing after another – gone as utterly as we ourselves shall shortly be gone like ghosts at cock-crow. [125]

W HAT IS A VILLAGE without its people? Nothing, just an empty shell. We may revere buildings and field patterns that have lasted longer than their creators, but unless we study the people who created them we are missing the vital ingredient of history that unites us all. Understanding our forbears is necessary for making sense of our present and – hopefully – paving the way for a better future.

When the first simple graveyard search facility was added to the history page of the village website, chitterne.com, it soon became apparent that many descendants of past Chitterne families were enthusiastic about tracing their forbears. Many, who had previously lived here or spent time here, expressed a deep affection for the village. It was this enthusiasm that led my daughter Mandy and I to create the Chitterne People page for the website and since then the response has been overwhelming from all over the world.

The substance of this chapter is the result of information that has flowed into my computer via email from people connected with Chitterne's past, since the advent of that particular page. It has given me great pleasure to re-unite long lost relatives or to introduce descendants of the same family to each other for the first time, and in turn, people have been generous with the results of their research, which informs us here. The rest is thanks to the generosity of the present villagers or ex-villagers, who have freely given up their time to regale me with stories, comments and opinions, written and spoken.

Before embarking in earnest on the families and characters of Chitterne I will interject with a curious phenomenon that may provide food for thought: I was surprised when I first noticed a tomb bearing my family name of Ingram in St Mary's graveyard. Not a very common name, or so I thought, but since then I have taken note of how many other newcomers to the village bear the surnames of Chitterne families of old. Why should this be? Are people returning to their roots in Chitterne, or is it coincidence? Mine must be a coincidence; as yet I have found no connection to the William Ingram in the handsome table tomb, who, incidentally, was a farmer who died in 1843.

To illustrate the point here are some names of present or recent villagers, with the dates of their earlier namesakes in the village:

Coles: The will of Agnes Coles of Chitterne All Saints was dated 1597; the family were here until 1902.

Moody: Edmund Moody was elected registrar of both parishes in 1654, the family were here until 1967.

Morgan: In the 15th century the chief tenants of the Abbess of Lacock were the Morgan family. Edward Morgan founded a chantry chapel in All Saints in 1529. Thomas Morgan was a grocer in the village in the 18th century and Robert Morgan, the village police constable in 1900, died here in 1926.

Naish: Richard Naish, a wheelwright, came here from Hampshire in 1755, the family stayed until about 1970.

Northeast: there had been Northeasts in Chitterne from before 1700 until 1920, Charles Northeast, a carpenter, married Hannah Compton in 1738; William Northeast died 1920.

Pryor: William Pryor of Chitterne St Mary died in 1587; another William Pryor was a tobacco pipe maker the following century. This family appeared to have died out in the village with the death of yet another William in 1717.

Turner: Humphrey Turner, a yeoman farmer, was assessed for taxes here in 1648. His descendants remained in Chitterne All Saints farming until the following century. George Turner was the landlord of the King's Head in 1927.

Woods: Robert Woods was a butcher in Chitterne in 1699; he died in 1740.

To return to the long established families who have deep connections with the village and with each other; we shall see how the farming families intermarried in the chapter on farming, the farmworkers and craftsmen likewise and to some extent the non-conformists sought spouses amongst their own too.

Of the long established farming families only the Wallis family remain. They are connected by marriage to the Webster and Lavington families of Clump Farm, the Long family once of Chitterne Farm, the Comptons late of the Gate House and Glebe Farm, and the Titt family of Elm Farm.

Of the many families of farmworkers, craftsmen and tradesmen who once populated the village, there are descendants of the Poolmans, the Ashleys, the Grants, the Poldens, the Felthams, the Windsors and the Georges still living in the village.

There have been Wallises in Chitterne since the 17th century and in The Manor at Chitterne St Mary for over 150 years. But the present family are descended from William Wallis (c1774-1825) a farmer of Thatcham, Berkshire who came here in 1823.

William's wife was Mary Buckeridge, a relative of Sir Thomas White, a founder of St John's College, Oxford, and John Buckeridge, Bishop of Ely and college president. Through this association descendants are entitled to a founder's kin scholarship to that college, should they be sufficiently academic. This gift is sealed by the addition of the name 'Buckeridge' at baptism.

William and Mary had eleven children. Only second son William Wallis (1805-1884), their daughter Eliza and their son Peter remained in Chitterne. William farmed, Eliza married John Titt of Elm Farm and produced John Wallis Titt, of whom more later, and Peter died aged 17 after a riding accident. Five brothers emigrated to North America and one became a Methodist Minister and married Emily Lavington whose brother farmed at Clump Farm.

The second William Wallis rented Chitterne St Mary Manor and 460 acres of land from Walter Long, Lord of the Manor, in 1851. He became a brewer and maltster, landlord of the local public house, the King's Head, and grew barley. He was a churchwarden, overseer of guardians and surveyor of highways. He and his wife Mary White had seventeen children prompting the statement: 'there are enough Wallises and Bazells to make a football team'.[126] The Bazells were a family from Clump Farm. They had 13 children.

Thomas and Mark, two of William and Mary's sons went to North America but Mark returned and married Louisa the daughter of George and Elizabeth

Compton and farmed at Stapleford. Of their other sons, William farmed at Vernham Street, Hampshire; George at Thatcham, Berkshire; Archibald and Richard at various places in Wiltshire.[127]

William and Mary also raised two granddaughters, the daughters of their eldest daughter Mary Ann who had married George Langford and died young in America. George brought the two little girls, Alice and Louisa, back to the Manor to live with their grandparents, and then he returned to the USA, remarried and started a new family. Alice and Louisa were never to see their father again. Letters they wrote to him asking when they were to meet their new mother and new little brother were carefully kept by the new family,[128] but their dreams were never realised. Alice became a governess and remained single in Chitterne, while Louisa married James Coles, a farmer, and lived at Brixton Deverill and Winterbourne Stoke.

The Manor at Chitterne passed to one of the second William's younger sons, Frederick Buckeridge Wallis (1858-1941). He and his wife Ellen had nine children, one of whom was killed in World War 1. After the war Frederick initiated the purchase of The Manor from Walter Long with a mortgage that wasn't paid off until the next generation. His two youngest sons, Victor and Donald, stayed in Chitterne.

Victor, father of the present owner, took on The Manor and paid off the mortgage. He formed another farming alliance by marrying Winifred Webster of Clump Farm. He died in 1962 aged 64 and Winifred in 1973 aged 71. Donald took on Glebe Farm, which the Wallis family also owned. Donald died in 1952.

The Compton family had been established in Chitterne longer than the Wallises when the last member of their family in Chitterne, Ann Compton, died in 1931. They probably came to Chitterne All Saints after King Henry VIII took back the Lacock Abbey lands in 1543. John and Avis Compton both paid benevolence to the King in 1545, and in 1576 another John Compton paid tax on profits to King Henry's daughter, Queen Elizabeth.[129]

The Comptons continued to be well-to-do farmers, authors of the Chitterne Glebe Terriers and provided churchwardens for many a generation. John Compton was a churchwarden in 1754 when new bells were cast and his name is engraved on the tenor and number 4 bells still in use today.

One branch of the family continued to live in The Gate House, another branch moved to Chitterne St Mary where they became maltsters. Thomas Compton and his wife Mary Burbidge built a house and a malthouse, supposedly in Bidden Lane,[130] which was taken over by Antony Burbidge[131] when Thomas died in 1785.

A tea party on the Tithing Field in 1911. From the left: Nora Feltham; unknown; unknown; Beryl Feltham; unknown; unknown; Harold Down; Esme Feltham; Alma Feltham (née Polden); unknown; unknown; unknown; unlnown; Annie Compton?

Charles Compton leased Bridge Cottage, he was born about 1750 and became a baker. James Compton, a shoemaker, lived there in 1842 and succeeding generations until Ann Compton, spinster, was the only Compton left. Not the shy retiring type and described as 'a unique Chitterne character' and 'England's oldest councillor' by the local paper, she certainly ended the Chitterne Compton dynasty on a high note. We will digress from families briefly and look at Annie's life in more depth.

Ann Compton, or preferably Annie, was the only woman on the new Warminster Rural District Council at its inception in 1894, where she represented Chitterne St Mary. By virtue of her place on the council she was also a member of the Board of Guardians of Warminster Workhouse. She was still serving on the Board when it was disbanded in 1930 and attended the final meeting in Warminster at the age of 90. The newspaper account best sums up her life:

> In her 92nd year, Miss Ann Compton passed away at Chitterne on Sunday . . . She was a link between the Early Victorian age and the Modern Age and she was always proud of the great character that brought fame to England in her childhood days.

Miss Compton was a striking personality with remarkable gifts . . . One of the good 'old-fashioned school', Miss Compton was a human 'land-mark' in Chitterne for generations whose advice was often sought and who was regarded as everybody's friend . . . She had one brother who farmed at Glebe Farm, Chitterne and two sisters – Mrs Mark Wallis, of Stapleford, and Mrs Guy, of London. Miss Compton devoted nearly forty years of her life in the interest of the community . . . When Miss Compton first became a councillor, mode of transport was not quite as comfortable as the modern system, and it is recorded that on occasions she has walked nine miles to attend the Board meetings at Warminster. For many years, she walked three miles to Codford Station en route to the Council meetings, and then walked the same three miles home in the evening . . . a striking contrast to the type of character that is in the majority today . . . Perhaps but few of the present generation knew that Miss Compton . . . was a staunch Liberal in politics . . . (She) once lived away from Chitterne, for a short period – when she was a school teacher in London – (and) had for some years entertained many villagers to tea on the occasion of her birthday. She was well read in history, and always proud of the history of Chitterne . . [132]

Understanding the family alliances we have looked at so far, within the farming community, has been simple when compared with the convoluted tapestry of marriages between the remaining Chitterne folk. I am not going to attempt to unravel the tapestry, suffice it to say that descendants of old Chitterne families here today are most certainly related to each other. We will concentrate instead on the provenance of the old families still represented in the village: the Ashley, Feltham, George, Grant, Poolman, Polden, and Windsor families.

Ancestors of the Ashley, Grant and Poolman families all arrived in the village in the 1700s when farmwork was abundant. Coincidentally all three families leant towards non-conformism, as we have already seen with the Grant family in the chapter called Praying and Learning, and all were related through marriage.

There were many William Ashleys; the first was William Aishley (original spelling) who married Chitterne-born Elizabeth Hart. William was born about 1776, but not in Chitterne, and his descendants live here still, though none bearing the Ashley name.[133]

The Chitterne Grant dynasty started with John Grant who was born about 1660 and married Sarah Titt in 1691; they spawned the many Grant families who lived in Chitterne down the years. The early generations were quite well-to-do, they leased land and farmed[134] but later most worked on the land, some were carriers and the grandfather of a descendant living in the village now, was a lengthman.[135]

Six generations of the Poolman family descended from John Poolman and Betty Eyles who were married in 1757 have lived in Chitterne; many by tradition were shepherds; other descendants are scattered across Hampshire, Dorset, Somerset, Berkshire, Sussex and Northamptonshire.[136]

William Windsor, who died in 1789, and his son William, who married Ann Smith and produced eleven children, were both blacksmiths. Third generation Elizabeth Windsor married Robert Poolman, son of the John Poolman and Betty Eyles mentioned previously, and had eight children, two of whom married members of the Grant family. George Poolman married Sarah Grant and John Poolman married Elizabeth Grant. Later members of the Windsor family were farmworkers but when William Windsor, born about 1864, married Ada Harriet Polden daughter of the stonemason Abdon Polden, he started a new line of builders that continues to this day.[137]

Abdon Polden's family at Alma Cottage c.1905. Abdon is in the centre leaning on the barrel of beer; his granddaughter Beryl Feltham is fourth from left back row; her mother Alma Feltham (née Polden) is eighth; Beryl's sisters Nora and Esme are second and third from left in the front row.

The earliest member of the Polden (earlier spelling: Polten) family in Chitterne I have found is John Polden, born about 1775 in Chitterne St Mary, but I am sure the family has been here longer than that. James Polden, born 1804, was Parish Clerk for at least 20 years from about 1830; he was the father of Abdon Polden, the stonemason, who deserves more than a few words to sum up his achievements.

Abdon Polden was born in 1835, the third child of James and Susannah Polden, a literate family. From the age of 11 he worked primarily on the properties owned by Walter Long, Lord of the Manor, in the village, and probably learned his trade under the stonemasons employed by Long. By the age of 26 he was overseer of the masons building the new village church[138] and was involved with the demolition of the two old churches. He installed the original door to the Michell's pew from old All Saints Church in his own house, Alma Cottage, at the top of the stairs.[139]

In recognition of his long service he was presented with an inlaid mahogany clock, inscribed: 'Presented by the Right Honourable Walter Hume Long M.P. to Abdon Polden, after sixty two years of faithful service on the Chitterne Estates. March 1906.'[140]

In his spare time Abdon was bandmaster of Chitterne Brass Band, organist at the church, a role he fulfilled for 50 years, and, along with his wife Jane, a member of the church choir throughout his life. His distinctive appearance: bearded, bowler-hatted and sporting a single black eyepatch over his left eye, means he is easily spotted on photographs of the band. His service to the choir is commemorated on his tombstone in All Saints graveyard; Abdon Close in Chitterne is a more obvious memorial to him and was built on a field he owned. He died in 1924 aged 89 years.

In 1878 Abdon Polden's son Clement started a carpenter and wheelwright company called Polden and Feltham with his brother-in-law Jimmy Feltham, which brings us neatly to the Feltham family.

In the Chitterne church registers the spelling of the name Feltham seems to have caused some trouble. In 1783 on 25th June the baptism is recorded of Mary, daughter of John and Betty 'Veltem'. In 1786 the name is spelt 'Voltum'.[141] However, the Feltham family thrived throughout the 19th and 20th centuries. Among their number were traders as well as craftsmen and the inevitable agricultural workers. Herbert Feltham was a general dealer and Thomas Feltham a butcher. But perhaps the most remarkable was Jimmy Feltham.

William James Cockrell Feltham, known as Jimmy, son of William Feltham and Maria Cockrell, was born in 1857. He was one half of Polden and Feltham, and married to Alma Polden, daughter of Abdon and Jane. Although by trade a carpenter, in his heart he was a soldier.

Jimmy was one of the 'Old Wiltshire Volunteers' and was said to have had a record of volunteer service that was second to none in the whole of the country.[142] The Volunteers had a base at Warminster where they trained two nights a week. Always smartly turned out in his scarlet tunic, pill-box hat, dark blue trousers, polished boots, waxed moustache and with his swagger cane tucked under his arm, Jimmy marched the eight miles to Warminster, trained his men for an hour and marched back to Chitterne

William James Cockrell Feltham's family c.1898. From the left: Geoffrey; Nora; Esme; Jimmy; Alma; Beryl and Evelyn.

again. He marched the choirboys at the church to their places in the choir stalls of a Sunday and started a Young Men's Club that he ran until World War II.[143] He gave the land at the bottom of Bidden Lane for the Village Hut to be erected on in 1921[144] and was also the parish clerk. He died at the age of 92 years in 1949.

The George family were carriers; James George, born 1787, was a carrier in Chitterne All Saints in 1851.[145] By 1875 the family had become beer retailers and bakers as well as carriers at The White Hart Inn.[146] But Thomas George c1780-1850 was a builder. He was involved with converting the old Mansion House stables into farmworkers' dwellings after the house was demolished in the 1820s.

Luckily for those of us interested in history the George family has a tradition of recording and preserving details of everyday village life as it happens around them. Thomas the builder was also a more than competent artist with a pencil, and he took the time to record a view of Chitterne seldom seen while he was aloft in the old stables. Other members of the George family were competent writers and have left behind vivid descriptions of life in old Chitterne, such as ten-year-old Olivia George's excellent essay of 1887, which is brilliantly evocative of that era.

Edwin George born in Chitterne in 1872, found work as a carter with the Great Western Railway in Bristol in 1900 when farm work was unobtainable in the village. He passed on his memories of old Chitterne orally to his nephew, Ernie George who, again luckily for us, combined the family traditions and not only recorded them on paper but illustrated them too.

Now we must consider three Chitterne-born or bred characters who made a name for themselves elsewhere. Whose families were not necessarily long established in the village, but were based here at the time of their offspring's success. The first of these is Percy Dean a descendant of the Deans of Imber.

Joseph Percy Dean was the son of farmers, Joseph and Louisa Dean of Chitterne Farm, but Percy, as he was always known, was not destined to be a farmer. He had a passion for motors. In 1902 he provided most of the capital of £3800 for a new venture with William and Albert Burden, previously clockmakers, to make motor engines. A new company was founded called Dean and Burden Brothers, motor engineers. Their premises were the Excelsior Works in the Friary, Salisbury, where clockmaking continued as well as the manufacture of motorboat and motorcycle engines. Percy Dean became a director of the company and their chief test driver.

In 1904 the company name was changed to Scout Motors and the following year their marine engines began to win accolades. Percy Dean took first, second and third places in races at Cowes, Ryde and Southampton Water in a 12 hp boat.

The first car was produced in 1905. It was entered in the Isle of Man Tourist Trophy Race with Percy Dean driving, but it went off the road at Wallop on the way there and was unplaced. Despite this setback the firm was soon busy with orders and was notable as the only sizeable local industry. In Chitterne Polden and Feltham owned a Scout vehicle.

In 1906 Percy Dean was awarded an Automobile Club of Great Britain medal for coming 9th out of 26 starters at the Isle of Man Tourist Race. The factory in the Friary became too small and in 1907 the company moved to new premises built for them on the Bemerton Road at Churchfields.

Percy Dean drove the Scout car entered in the Isle of Man TT Race again in 1908 but the car ran out of petrol less than a 100 metres from the finish. The first Scout commercial vehicle, a motor delivery van, was produced in 1909 and production of marine engines stopped. For two years the company's sales increased, then in 1911 Percy Dean left to go to British Columbia. In his leaving speech he showed foresight when he mentioned the competition facing the company from foreign firms, for in 1921, having survived the hard times of World War 1, the company went into voluntary liquidation.

We have already met the parents of the next subject in another chapter. Bill Brown, or properly William Fred Brown. He was born in Chitterne in 1872 to Willam Frederick and Sarah Brown who lived at the Chitterne Post Office, 53 Bidden Lane (Shrewton Road). Bill's Chitterne childhood fitted him for the most unlikely of jobs, that of the Chief of CID at Scotland Yard. His father, besides being the postmaster was also the Headmaster of the local school and his mother was Assistant Mistress.

Young Fred and his three older sisters, Rosa, Annie and Mary, were taught at their father's school. At 18 Bill went to London where he joined the Metropolitan Police on 5 February 1894 as PC 172 in M Division (Lambeth). He rose spectacularly through the ranks to Detective Inspector, then to Detective Chief Superintendent in charge of CID headquarters at Scotland Yard. As such he was one of the 'Big 5'. (The Big Five was the newspaper journalists' nickname for the Detective Chief Superintendents in charge of the four London Districts in the Metropolitan Police, plus their colleague in charge of CID HQ in Scotland Yard, when he was raised to their rank in 1921).[147] Bill was responsible for solving some of the most notorious crimes that happened in London at the time, and for arresting murderers such as Ronald True, who murdered a woman in her London flat.

Bill retired from the Metropolitan Police on 8 August 1932 as Detective Superintendent CO/C1. He was 59 years old and was awarded the M.B.E. in recognition of his 38 years of service.[148] He and his wife Mary retired to Chitterne, where they had always spent their annual holidays with Bill's sister Rosa. They bought the row of terraced cottages in Bidden Lane, including the cottage where Bill had lived as a boy, which they mostly had demolished, except for Fred's old home, which was incorporated into a new house. They called the new house 'Syringa Cottage'. Besides pottering in his garden, Bill was a Justice of the Peace, a Parish Councillor and helped with village events. He died suddenly in 1941, aged 68, when helping to find billets for the evacuees arriving from London. He and his wife are buried in St Mary's graveyard.

John Wallis Titt, our third successful person, is a descendant of the Titt family who farmed here for several generations having originally arrived in the village as blacksmiths from Wylye in the 18th century. John was a result of the union of John Titt and Eliza Wallis, who lived and farmed at Elm Farm. He was born in 1841 at The Manor, Chitterne St Mary, as were all Eliza's children.

As a youngster helping his father on Elm Farm it was one of John's jobs to look after the family's windmill.[149] This early experience eventually led to the formation of his internationally known company, John Wallis Titt. In 1865 he left Elm

John Wallis Titt and family c.1888. Back row: Edith; Florence; Herbert. Middle row: Helen; Wallis (Jack); John Wallis Titt; Amy; Emily Eliza Titt (née Sainsbury); Harold; Alec Buckeridge. Front: Ethel (Kitty).

Farm to work as a commercial traveller for Wallis, Haslan and Stevens in Basingstoke, they made agricultural implements and steam engines. In 1867 he joined Brown and May of Devizes, a firm of millwrights. In 1872 he started his own business in Portway, Warminster as an agricultural engineer mostly making hay and straw elevators and acting as an agent for mowers and reapers.

In 1876 he moved to Woodcock, Warminster and established the Woodcock Iron Works, carrying on as agricultural engineers and founders. The first pumps the company made were for the Boyton estate in the Wylye Valley in 1884, probably also the date of the first John Wallis Titt wind engines. By 1885 they were producing annular-sailed windmills; the Woodcock wind pumping engine, the Simplex direct wind pumping engine and the Simplex geared wind engine were their most important products.[150] Polden Brothers builders, of Chitterne, built many of the bases for the wind engines in England and abroad.

John Wallis Titt died in 1910 and his sons carried on the business they had been running since 1903 when he first became ill.

Lastly a look at the achievements of a man who came to Chitterne as an adult and made a name for himself, not only in the village but all over the Salisbury Plain. His name: Frank Maidment.

Frank Maidment was a giant of a man both in stature and in achievement. Tall and jovial, and known to his

Frank Maidment.

friends as the 'Bishop' of Salisbury Plain, he had many talents: a Baptist preacher, a baker, sub-postmaster, village shopkeeper and publisher of postcards. When he died in 1952, he had spent an incredible 75 years preaching the Gospel. He preached at Chitterne and surrounding villages on the Plain for over 50 years, and from 1907 until 1943 he was the regular preacher at Imber, cycling there in the early days.

Born at Burcombe near Wilton in 1860 Frank came to Chitterne in 1881 to take over Jacob Everly's bakery and grocery business next door to the Baptist Chapel in Bidden Lane; later adding the village Post Office to the business. He was already a Wesleyan Methodist lay preacher.

As a baker, Frank was known for delivering verbal quotes from the Bible with his loaves. In his pony and trap he delivered bread around the village, to the field-barn cottages and even out as far as Imber. Frank always added a comment from the scriptures to his greeting as he handed out the loaves: 'Lovely day, Martha, Praise the Lord,' or 'Filthy day Bertha, work of the devil.'

Frank encouraged or admonished young and old alike, as he considered necessary. Viscount Long of Wraxall recalled, in a letter to him many years later:

> Well do I remember baking the loaves as a boy and generally making myself an infernal nuisance to you. But you always had a smile and you allowed us to play havoc in your shop. What happy days those were.

But to a parent of a youth he considered wayward Frank might say:

It grieves me to see fine village lads, your ***** among them, loafing at the bottom of the lane, wi' their hands in their pockets. Mark my words; nothing good will come of it. Idle hands make idle minds. Six days shalt thou labour.

It was not unknown for him to stop on his way to his next preaching engagement and admonish any villager he found working on a Sunday, and ask them why they were not at Chapel. For despite being a Weslyan, he continued his preaching at the Chitterne Baptist Chapel almost as soon as moving in next-door and he took the shepherding of his flock very seriously, gaining a reputation for his good work amongst the poor and sick. He and Rose were baptized in 1889 and Frank was made Deacon and asked to take a monthly service that same year. He became leader in 1904.

In 1932, in recognition of 50 years service at Chitterne Baptist Chapel, Frank was presented with a testimonial, in appreciation of his 'Loving and Devoted Service', and many gifts. In 1933 he was President of the Wiltshire and East Somerset Baptist Association. He was again praised after 60 years service as a lay preacher in Corton, Tilshead, Imber, Shrewton, Lavington, Littleton Panell, Crockerton, Westbury, Heytesbury and Westbury Leigh as well as Chitterne. He must have baptised, married and buried hundreds of people and travelled hundreds of miles in the course of his career.

Frank Maidment felt the loss of Imber, when it was requisitioned by the War Department in 1943, very keenly. He had been leader of the Baptist Chapel there for many years. He corresponded with Viscount Long and AG Street who, like him, did their utmost to have the village returned to the villagers at the end of the Second World War, but to no avail.

In 1949 Frank retired from his duties as sub-postmaster after 42 years of service to the villagers of Chitterne. He was 89 years old!

At the end of November 1952 Frank's second wife Annie died suddenly, aged 67 years. Frank himself was an invalid by this time and he died only 18 days later, on December 16th, 1952. He was 92 years old.[151] His tombstone says: 'A Faithful Baptist Preacher for 75 years at Chitterne and villages on Salisbury Plain.'

Farming

1851: total population of Chitterne 691; 7 farmers, 172 farm workers.
2001: total population of Chitterne 298; 3 farmers; 4 farm workers.

F ARMING has been the main reason for Chitterne's existence, until comparatively recently. Since the arrival here of the Neolithic barrow-builders who first controlled plant growth and the reproduction of animals, the surrounding area has been farmed. That is, for over 5000 years. Who could imagine the village without its regularly changing backdrop of brown, green and golden fields? Chitterne would not be the place it is were it not for the generations of folk who have worked the land. In the past the whole of village life revolved around the agricultural cycle and most families were involved in farming. Other services in the village existed just to satisfy their needs. This is not true today, so we will be looking into farming and how it has changed in Chitterne in detail. First, a look at how farming practice has changed through the years.

For several millennia only the upland areas were farmed and inhabited. Patterns of old field systems can still be seen at Chitterne Ansty, and between Chitterne and Maddington. At some stage people started to settle in the valleys and cultivate the lower ground. Eventually there were small farmsteads with crops grown in garden sized plots and grazing livestock, moved to higher ground in summer, a regime that lasted for many centuries.[152] Signs of old cultivation in the village existed in living memory; a steep slope behind Chitterne Farm Cottages had a series of terraces called linches; these were levelled when the farm cottages were built. The track that passes in front of the cottages was known locally as Linches Path.[153]

The linches on Chitterne Farm land that were bulldozed to make way for Chitterne Farm Cottages.

The Romans made little impact on farming here. They favoured the high ground for settlements and continued the agricultural practice already in place, possibly expanding output to feed their army. The Saxons introduced sheep farming, the most successful use yet of the chalkland. They also organised the family farmsteads into 'hundreds'. Chitterne was part of the Heytesbury Hundred. By the time of the Norman Domesday Survey in 1086, Chitterne boasted 2620 acres of ploughland, and 26 acres of meadow and pasture, farmed under the feudal system with 12 slaves, 11 freedmen, 19 villagers, 6 cottagers and 2 smallholders. Chitterne's isolation probably meant that this system continued until about 1500, longer than in other places, where expectation of labour was commuted for a payment of money from around 1400, and the lord only claimed a week's work in summer and autumn for haymaking and harvest.

Apart from the Domesday Survey there are few historical facts available until the Prior of Bradenstoke took over the Manor of Chitterne All Saints. Under the Priory's care the Manor lands grew from half a hide in 1184 until, in 1291, the estate included extensive pasture for sheep and was worth £3.5s.6d.[154] Likewise, the nuns of Lacock also owned much Chitterne land, confirmed by Henry III in 1247. The nuns managed their lands and farms in Chitterne on a commercial basis. They sold surplus produce once their own needs had been met, actively sought to increase their acreage of pasture and reared sheep to sell for profit. Sheep fairs were held at Yarnbury Castle not far distant. The nuns' portion of the produce from Chitterne land was almost a third in 1341, in fact Chitterne was more valuable to the nuns than Lacock itself.

Over time the sheep and corn farming regime had become refined, where the sheep fed on the down during the day and were folded at night in rotation on the arable land growing cereal crops, to provide much needed manure. By about 1325 there was a windmill for grinding the corn, sited on Windmill Hill, Chitterne All Saints.[155] The nuns unfree tenants were responsible for washing and shearing the sheep; the fleeces were sold for more profit or sent to one of the abbey's fulling mills for processing. In 1476 the nuns owned a flock of over 2000 sheep tended by shepherds who had defined duties and privileges.

Gradually the commercial exploitation of Chitterne land by the nuns decreased. At the dissolution the nuns' flock at Chitterne consisted of 600 wethers,

The water meadows in 1901.

600 ewes and 300 hogs and the customary tenants were still washing and shearing them.

After the dissolution the new owners kept to the same regime. William Jordan, principal farmer in Chitterne All Saints, left his wife a store of wool, sheep, 'corne of all sorts', horse and oxen, rams and 'hogsheepe' at Chitterne that wintered elsewhere, and the 'occupacion and proffytt of all my lands and ffarmes in Chitterne'.[156]

Until the mid 17th century the only stumbling block to increased production of wool and cereals was the lack of early pasture for the sheep. A groundbreaking innovation in farming practice overcame this: meadows were 'floated', that is, the low-lying meadows were flooded during the winter months. A procedure that produced

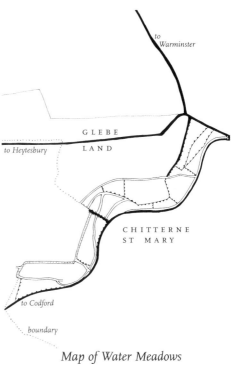

Map of Water Meadows

more grass for the sheep, thereby allowing more sheep to be kept and so more crops to be manured by them. This system was developed not far from Chitterne, in the Wylye valley, on the Earl of Pembroke's land.

The old water meadows in Chitterne St Mary, alongside the road to Codford, operated in this way. The dykes took a week to fill when the hatches were lowered to allow flooding from the Chitterne Brook.[157] At one time each farmer in Chitterne had a part of the meadow for his own use and so could benefit from the extra fodder. Each part bore the name of its farmer owner but the names have since been lost except for one, 'Dean's Meadow'. Later the parts were reunited as part of Glebe Farm, as they are today. The hatches have long since disappeared, along with the hedgerows that divided the farmers' plots.[158]

With larger flocks of sheep, usually Hampshire Down, providing more manure, areas of higher ground were brought under cultivation and Field Barn settlements were established on remote parts of extensive farms to cut down on travelling time for the farm workers. The settlements were up to two and a half miles from the village and included up to five cottages and a bailiff's house, stables for 10 or 12 horses as well as the barn for storing corn, all often encircled by trees on the northern and eastern sides for protection from the wind. It was a very isolated life. The workers may have been nearer to their jobs but, come the 19th century and compulsory education, the children had to trek up to two and a half miles to school, often along deep muddy tracks in winter.

With farming becoming more profitable, although the number of gentleman farmers and employers of numerous waged farm workers increased, the number of family and part-time farmers decreased, almost ending a tradition that dated back to Norman and possibly pre-Saxon times. Despite the new profit-driven farming practices, farmers and tenants were still subject to husbandry regulations enforced by manorial courts, a system dating from feudal times, where property and land was leased for three lives. This carried on until at least 1800 in Chitterne, but family farmers now frequently mortgaged their copyholds for life, and often failed to add a new life at the death of one of the life-holders. The final blows to family farmers came with inclosure in 1815 followed by mechanisation. But as usual, given its isolation, in Chitterne things were slow to change and horses were still used on farms here until World War II.

The profitable times for gentleman farmers did not last long. The cheap grain imports allowed by the repeal of the Corn Laws, led to an agricultural depression; much of the cultivated high land reverted to grass and surplus farm workers were so poor and starving that many were forced to leave the land, and some even the country. In 1840 Cornelius and Mary Polden quit England completely and set sail for a new life in Australia, as did John and Charlotte Foyle in 1847.

At the end of the 19th century a series of very wet cold summers and low grain yields compounded the problem and the use of artificial fertilisers meant that sheep were no longer needed for their manure; gradually cattle and a few pigs replaced the sheep on most farms. Before this no cows were kept in great numbers, just the few kept by farmers for their own family. They would sell skim milk for 1d. a quart, or new milk for 1½d. Basic farm wages were 8s. or 9s. a week for a man, and a woman worked on the farm for 6d. a day, starting at 6 am.

Farmworkers lived in rows of cottages, like those in Bidden Lane, where rents in the early 1900s were 1 shilling a week, this included a piece of land where the family could grow their own vegetables or keep chickens. The chief farm crops were wheat, oats and barley, but the highest paid work was turnip hoeing and it attracted men from as far away as Bristol, but the season was short. Next most profitable was harvesting. With a combination of turnip hoeing and harvesting, it was possible to earn 14 or 15 shillings a week, which averaged at 10 or 11 shillings over the year.[159] By 1914, with fewer men available, basic wages had risen to 10s. or 12s. a week.[160]

Farmwork was still hard manual work at this time in Chitterne. The corn was harvested in the traditional way by hand, using sickles and bound into sheaves tied with ropes of twisted straw. The sheaves were flailed, and winnowed in the farmyards by hand, usually by women, then the corn gathered in sacks and stored in barns. The stalks were built into a round rick, with a thatched 'roof' ready for use as animal bedding, or thatching wall-tops. With the arrival of mechanisation about 30 years later, the corn was cut, gathered into sheaves, bound, and dropped, all in one operation by a binder-machine drawn by two large horses. The sheaves were later stacked into hiles, a local term for a stook, by hand.

George Bailey mowing on Chitterne Farm 1930s.

Children were always employed on the farms at busy times such as harvest, haymaking or potato planting. This continued even after school attendance became compulsory. Children were employed to help with the harvest at least until World War II. If harvest was late the farmer would apply to the schools for the children to be excused lessons for an extra week to help finish the harvesting.

At harvest time the older boys aspired to be picked as leaders. Leaders led the shire-type horses pulling the trailer around the field from hile to hile, collecting sheaves until the trailer was full, then they led the horses to the rick being built to unload, then on round again collecting sheaves and so on. At the end of the day they put the horses away, brushed them down and washed and brushed their feet. A far more exciting way to spend the summer than learning lessons.[161] 'When there was any fun going, any coursing on the Downs, or rats to be killed when a rick was being thrashed, the farmers sent for us.'[162]

George Bailey and his son Bert c. who both worked on Chitterne Farm.

Each season brought its traditional farming practice. Late Spring meant rook shooting, when parties of farmers, with guns and young boys to carry the bags of cartridges and collect the dead birds, gathered at Claypits Clump, Gasson or the Hollow supposedly to rid the area of rooks and jackdaws. Beech and horse chestnut treetops would be black with dozens of bird's nests. The idea was to kill the parent birds and thereby kill the nestlings by starvation. But despite the rook shoot there would be just as many nests the next year.

The threshing season meant excitement among the children when the traction engine towing a threshing machine trundled through the village. Following along behind came a cartload of coal and a barrel full of water, and keeping up alongside as word got around, a growing band of children. The boys looking forward to the 'ratting' as the ricks were demolished, which they accomplished standing in a circle wielding stout sticks, with the help of the foreman's ferocious terrier dog.

> In those days there was no wire upon the Downs, just as there were no fences or ditches. All was open. You could ride N.S.E. or W. as you willed. In three directions from Chitterne you could ride at least ten miles without ever being off the grass, except for one or two quite short bits of hard road. We were able to see something of

A shooting party at Manor Farmhouse c.1900.

hawking. Major Fisher of Stroud came year by year to Chitterne to hawk rooks in the spring and partridges in the autumn . . . Another sportsman who came to Chitterne was Mr Mitchell, who hawked larks with merlins . . . we enjoyed the sport with merlins as it was not necessary to be mounted. All that was required was keen eyes and a good pair of legs.[163]

None of these practices happen nowadays since the advent of fully mechanised harvesting and threshing; even the rooks are left in peace. Farms are seen as dangerous places for children, except for those that open up on display for visitors, what a sea-change from less than a lifetime ago.

Charles Churchill driving a Titan tractor at Clump Farm in 1926.

Two other major changes have happened to farming in Chitterne in the last 50 years, surely the biggest and fastest changes to date. They are the decrease in the number of village people employed in agriculture, and the consolidation in the number of separate farms.

First, the field barn settlements started to be abandoned from the beginning of the 20th century. This process speeded up after the War Department purchased several thousand acres of farmland around Chitterne for training troops in the 1930s. They compulsorily purchased 3000 acres and farm buildings previously owned by R J Faquharson in 1937. Farm managers found themselves with a government department as landlord with new regulations and new categories of land. The outlying field barn settlements were in the way of troop training and by 1950 all the buildings had gone at Down Barn and New Barn. Breach Hill Farmstead was demolished and became the site of military vedette post number 4, which was in turn demolished in 2002. New Barn farmland and Middle Barn were absorbed into Chitterne Farm.

Chitterne Farm c.1955.

In 1955 there were still eight farms in the village, five of them owned by the War Department, and now in 2007 there are only three. Chitterne Farm has known the greatest change; over the period it has absorbed four of the other farms and the number of men employed on the farm has decreased from seven to only one. It seems incredible that one man can do the work formerly done by seven, but when the acreage has more than doubled at the same time, it is mind-boggling. 'With up-to-date machinery there is little need for more labour, except in emergencies and in the past several farmers have joined forces to help each other out as necessary'. [164]

Bert Bailey holding one of Fred Babey's bulls at Chitterne Farm c.1960s.

Possibly the major factor in this latter change is the disappearance since 1955 of the six dairy herds, comprising 440 cows; now there are none. The total number of farm workers employed in the village has also decreased in that time from 29 to 4.

> 'In the 1950s Codford railway station was still operating. Cattle were still transported by train. Truckloads of cattle came from Scotland to Codford station and were driven, on foot, to the local farms for fattening. Corn and cattle and pig feeds were also brought by rail and collected by the farmers with tractors and trailers. After the Salisbury markets on Tuesdays up to 100 cattle were driven through the streets of Salisbury to the goods station off the Southampton Road. None of this happens in 2000. [165]

Fred Babey firing the stubble at Chitterne Farm.

So what has happened to all the farmers, farm buildings and farmyards? We will look at each farm's history next.

History of the Farms – All Saints

The early history of the individual farms at All Saints concerns the nuns of Lacock and the prior of Bradenstoke. The Lacock records mention the East Farm, perhaps referring to Chitterne Farm. Perhaps the farm belonging to Bradenstoke, Manor Farm, was known as the West Farm, or Chitterne Farm (West), as it is today. We cannot be sure. We do know that The Gate House[166] seems to have been used as a farmhouse until the 20th century, likewise The Grange from c1800 for at least 100 years; Chitterne Lodge also until the early 20th century. Manor Farm, on the other side of the road is a little more straightforward.

The Abbess of Lacock's main customary tenants were the Morgan family, who probably lived on The Gate House site but also held other lands and tenements in both Chitternes. By 1517 the East Farm at Chitterne was leased with the nuns' pasture and flock. By 1535 all the nuns' pastures at Chitterne were let, and Henry VIII's survey noted a farm and a sheep-walk on land leased to the Morgans. The flock was sold to Thomas Temys in 1538 for £150, who also leased two farms formerly held by the nuns.

After Lacock Abbey and Bradenstoke Priory were dissolved the Compton family were tenant farmers, possibly under the Temys' and Jordans, but certainly under the Paulets, the Michells and Richard Hayward. They farmed from The Gate House, probably known as the East Farm.

Alfred Blake and his two sons George and Robert were tenant farmers of Walter Long at Chitterne Lodge from 1861 until the end of the century. George Blake, who married Elizabeth Hitchcock, of the Manor Farm Hitchcocks, farmed 1400 acres and his brother Robert 175 acres. The name of the farm is not known.

Joseph Dean and his family from Imber farmed 1250 acres and ran a large flock of Hampshire Down sheep[167] from The Grange in 1880 and the following year from Chitterne Farm.

Chitterne Farm: Chitterne Farmhouse was renovated in 1881 under the ownership of Walter Hume Long, following the death of his tenant, Edward Gibbs, in 1879. The Dean family farmed at Chitterne Farm until Walter Hume Long sold the farm and Chitterne Lodge to Ronald James Farquharson in 1906.

Farquharson employed Robert W. Long, a distant relative of W.H. Long, as his estate agent from 1908 to 1953. Robert Long had recently married Helen Wallis, of the Wallis family at The Manor. In the 1930s the War Department compulsorily purchased all RJ Farquharson's land and buildings. The Long family continued at Chitterne Farm

Eric Babey cutting grass on Chitterne Farm in 1984.

until Robert Long's death in 1953, when the old farm buildings were still intact.

On February 4th 1955 the Babey family arrived at Chitterne Farm, where seven men were employed. By 1984 the farm had absorbed four of the other seven farms in the village, Elm Farm, Middle Barn Farm, New Barn Farm and lastly, Manor Farm, which, like Chitterne Farm, were all owned by the Ministry of Defence, formerly the War Department. The much-enlarged Chitterne Farm is still intact today.

Elm Farm: In 1798 millwright William Watts of Great Cheverell built a windmill for grinding grain in Chitterne All Saints. It was of a timber and thatch post mill type with four sails and contained one pair of stones for grist and a pair of French stones. It stood alongside the farm track known as Tyning Path. In 1798 William insured it for £300 and his tenant was George Baker, but in 1799 it was up for sale with a store-house.

The farmhouse at Elm Farm, built in the first half of the 19th century, was probably the new house that was offered for sale with the windmill in 1831, after the death of the tenant miller, John Grant. John Grant was the maternal grandfather of John Titt, who married Eliza Wallis in 1831. By 1855 John Titt was the tenant miller and farmer[168] and lived at Elm Farm farming 220 acres. John Wallis Titt, his son the engineer, had charge of this windmill as a young man and it most probably inspired his later career as a specialist in windpumps. George Abery junior was the last recorded miller in Chitterne in 1859.

Elm Farm was back in the hands of the Baker family in 1881. In 1901 it was occupied by John and Alice Woodman. The Gagen family farmed Elm Farm during World War 1 and Percy Gagen in 1927.

After the farmland became part of Chitterne Farm the farmyard became the depot for the Defence Properties Service Agency, an agency that repaired and maintained MoD properties. At the end of the 20th century the depot was closed and the yard was sold for housing. The farmhouse had been sold earlier to a private buyer.

Manor Farm: The principal farm of the Manor of Chitterne All Saints was part of the estate of the Earls of Salisbury, until a member of that family gave the Manor to Bradenstoke Priory before 1184. By 1232 the priory had purposefully increased its acreage from half a hide to 'extensive pastures for sheep.' [169]

Early owners of this farm were also Lords of the Manor, whom we have already met. [170] The old farmhouse also featured extensively in our earlier village tour. [171] So, to avoid repetition I will merely list the holders of Manor Farm here:

Earls of Salisbury; Bradenstoke Priory; Temys 1545-1580; Jordan 1580-1662; Giles 1662-1710? Holder 1710?-1771; Methuen 1771-1815, Onslow-Michell c1815-1895; Collins 1895-1937; Ministry of Defence 1937-1984; farmland only: Ministry of Defence 1984- present.

The tenants of Manor Farm were possibly William Newman; William Tugwell in 1793, and John Kenton leased 1604 acres in 1806 for 21 years, Harry and Jane Hitchcock farmed 1656 acres in 1851. [172] In 1881 the Hitchcock women ran the farm of 1700 acres. [173] Led by Ann Hitchcock aged 26, and her four sisters; they employed 25 men and 6 boys. By 1890 the Cleverley brothers were tenants.

John Collins and his son Charles, farmers from Devon, owned and farmed Manor Farm 1895 – 1937. John Collins engaged John Wallis Titt to install a windpump to pump water for the farm in 1905. Charles Collins took over after his father retired; his farm bailiff was Robert Samuel Hiscock. [174] Charles Collins died in 1937 and the Farm was sold to the War Department.

Up to and during World War II Tom Limbrick was the tenant farmer. From October 1954 to 1984 brothers Michael and Roy Walker were the last tenants of Manor Farm before it was amalgamated with Chitterne Farm. In 1984, a few months before they fell victim to the slump in farming, the Walker brothers allowed a film company to film on Manor Farm land, at the site of the former Down Barn fieldbarn settlement. A crop of sweetcorn was grown to help create the illusion that Manor Farm was Kansas, USA, for the sequel to The Wizard of Oz, called Return to Oz. Later that year the estate was split, with the house and stables and paddock being sold off separately and the rest of the land becoming part of Chitterne Farm, known as Chitterne Farm West.

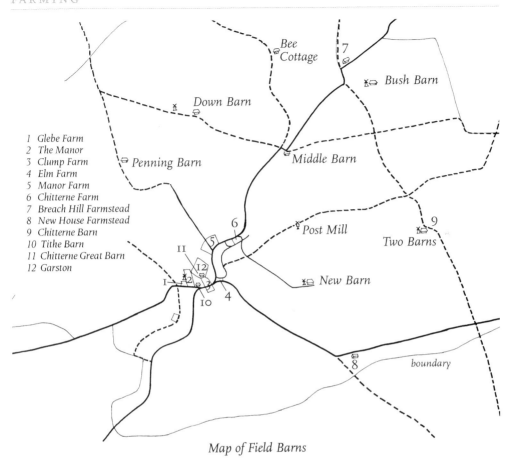

1 Glebe Farm
2 The Manor
3 Clump Farm
4 Elm Farm
5 Manor Farm
6 Chitterne Farm
7 Breach Hill Farmstead
8 New House Farmstead
9 Chitterne Barn
10 Tithe Barn
11 Chitterne Great Barn
12 Garston

Map of Field Barns

Field Barns, Farmsteads and Windmills at a distance from the Village:

Two Barns, New Barn, Bush Barn, Breach Hill Farmstead, Bee Cottage, Down Barn, Penning Barn, Middle Barn, New House Farm and Windmills 1 to 4 were the outlying field barn settlements and farmsteads associated with Chitterne. All were in All Saints parish.

Chitterne Barn, not to be confused with Chitterne Great Barn, was one of the barns at the Two Barns settlement. It was an agricultural masterpiece,[175] built in the early 18th century some way outside the village alongside the old road from Salisbury to Bath on land farmed at the time by the Michells. It was a thatched, six bay, timber-framed structure, built of solid oak. The centre legs were all cut from the same tree trunk, and all of the beams were numbered with Roman numerals and dowelled together. There is an interesting story attached to this historic building that we will come to in a later chapter.

At least four of John Wallis Titt's windpumps for pumping water were established in Chitterne early in the 20th century. Each required an attendant to live on site. In the event of strong winds the attendant could adjust the pitch of the blades to prevent the veins breaking up by turning too fast.[176] Of the windpumps within the parish boundary, four were still occupied in 1925.[177] Manor Farm's windpump, installed by John Wallis Titt for John Collins in 1905, was near the northern boundary of the parish to the west of Down Barn settlement. The remaining three windpumps were at Two Barns, New Barn and Bush Farm settlements.[178]

Bee Cottage: In Frying Pan Bottom, alongside the track to Imber; by World War 1 it was unoccupied.

Breach Hill Farmstead: Alongside the Tilshead road at the top of Breach Hill. It had two cottages, a barn, a cartshed and stables. In 1881 Joseph Ashley, agricultural labourer, lived in one cottage the other was uninhabited.

Bush Farm: On the opposite side of the Tilshead road to Breach Hill Farmstead, but further away from the road. There were two cottages and a windpump:

1 Arthur Ingram, carter 1881.

Widow Elizabeth Nash, her two sons, daughter and boarder Charles Musselwhite, in 1901.

2 Mary Waters, deserted by her agricultural labourer husband, in 1881.

Henry Page, carter 1901.

Harry Burton, gamekeeper 1925.

Down Barn: A field barn settlement and pond amongst beech trees near Breakheart Bottom. Only a few beech trees remain. Scenes from 'Return to Oz' were filmed there in 1984. Two cottages:

1 Uninhabited 1881. George Scott, carter 1901. Charles Barltrop left March 1923. Frederick Farr 1925.

2 William Light, carter 1881. Isaac Poolman, carter 1901. Reginald Scammell 1925.

Middle Barn Farmstead: At the bottom of Breach Hill, the only field barn settlement that still exists, but now part of Chitterne Farm. The semi-detached houses were built in 1915.

1 Edward Colley, shepherd 1901. Walter Herrington and William Maslen 1925.

2 Thomas Moody, carter 1901, Tom Bailey 1925.

New Barn: At the top of Long Hill, this settlement had stables, a wind-pump and five cottages:

1 Herbert Collins, shepherd 1901.

2 Charles Humphries, groom 1901.

3 William Farr, blacksmith 1901.

Two cottages empty 1901.

New House Farmstead: This small farm was outside the village at the top of Shrewton Hill. The redbrick farmhouse was demolished in the 1980s; only a timber shed remains.

Maurice Gagen left in October 1924.

Rev. Thomas Mason took over the same month.

Lewis Downs Mason farmed at New Farm 1927.

Jack Walberton farmed here in 1970s, 80s.

Penning Barn: In Breakheart bottom, a barn and cottage were sheltered by horse chestnut and hawthorn trees.

Robert Naish, carter 1881.

Walter Marshall, carter 1901.

Penning Cottage was unoccupied by World War 1.

Two Barns: Large field barn settlement on Copehill Down alongside the old Salisbury to Bath coach road. There were several cottages, two barns, a paddock , a windpump and a pig unit.

1 William Farr, journeyman blacksmith, 1881.

2 John Stokes, agric. Labourer, 1881.

3 Uninhabited 1881.

4 Tom Meade, shepherd, 1881.

5 James Cool, shepherd, 1881.

6 John Poolman, shepherd, 1881.

7 Alfred Tuffin, carter, 1881.

8 George Dewey, carter, 1881.

9 John Carter, bailiff, 1881.

Charles Munday, shepherd 1901.

Job Tilley, carter 1901.

3 houses empty 1901.

A house at Two Barns was destroyed by fire on the 9th June 1916.

Windmill 1: Edward Ings 1925.

Windmill 2

Elizabeth Nash, widow, formerly at Bush Farm, died 1916. Her daughter Louisa married the lodger Charles Musselwhite in 1918. Charles and Louisa still lived here in 1925.

Windmill 3

William Cox from 1913, 1925.

Windmill 4

William Nash 1925.

Bertram and Edward Polden were farmers in Chitterne 1927. They had a barn, stable and dairy about 100 metres along the Yarnbury track on the right. Eddie Polden lived in number 96 Chitterne.[179]

Henry John Smith 1901, 1927 farmed from numbers 79 and 80 at the top of Bidden Lane. He had a dairy building and a dewpond further up the Shrewton Hill on the right, and a cattle shelter on the Codford Road, where his cows roamed the old watermeadows.

St Marys

In Chitterne St Mary, as in Chitterne All Saints, most land and farms were held by Lacock Abbey before the dissolution. After the dissolution families called Milbourne and Flower were the principal landholders, followed by the Paulets, Methuens and Longs.

Very little is known of the Milbournes, beyond a mention in 1677 of the 'Milbourn farm flock'. Their tenants were the Imbers, who had previously been tenants of the nuns. John Imber had been bailiff of the Manor before the dissolution, and in 1532 he leased the South Farm from the nuns. South Farm may refer to Clump Farm or The Manor.

Thomas Flower lived, and kept a flock of sheep, in All Saints in 1588, but he also occupied part of an enclosure named Garston in St Mary. This is the field behind the sportsfield that stretches across both parishes. It contained the site of Chitterne's Great Barn, which we shall come to later. The Flowers' tenants were the Hayters.

The Hayter family were yeoman farmers and tenants of the Flowers for over 200 years. In 1620 Jordan Hayter of Chitterne St Mary married Margaret Flower of Imber, one of a series of farming alliances in the community. There is still a barn named Flowers' Field Barn at Chitterne Ansty, now converted into residential accommodation.

John Wallis, leased land and buildings from Norton Paulet in 1752 in Chitterne St Mary, including 'The Great Farm,' The Little Farm,' and 'Flemming's Bargain'. Paul Cobb Methuen bought these farms in 1808, but Flemming's Bargain was demolished in 1860.

Of the lands not owned by Lacock Abbey: the rectory or parsonage of Chitterne St Mary was held by the Dean and Chapter of Salisbury Cathedral, but there was no dwelling house attached, it consisted solely of land and a barn. The rectory lands were let to Jordan Slade in 1616 who lived in Chitterne All Saints and also had a house at Maddington. Several generations of the Slade family leased the rectorial lands and barn from the Dean and Chapter. A survey of those lands made in 1650 stated that:

'There is no Mansion or dwelling House. A Barn belonging to the said Parsonage of three Bays of Building standing and being on parcel of the Glebe Lands belonging to the Vicarage of Chitterne and adjoining to the Vicarage Barn worth per year 20s. There is belonging to the said Parsonage only the Tithe of all corn and grain grown and renewing within the said parish (except the Tithe of the Glebe Lands belonging to the Vicarage) which Tithe of the Parsonage aforesaid is worth per annum £49.'

The two barns mentioned in the extract above, both now gone, stood as follows: The Tithe Barn, between St Mary's church and the road on the site now partly occupied by Birch Cottage garage; the Great Barn, in Garston, as previously mentioned.

The Chitterne Great Barn, and associated large meadow, probably Garston, and a stockyard, possibly Clump Farm Pig Unit, now St Mary's Close, were part of the rectorial or parsonage estate. In the 17th/18th centuries the rectory barn stood beside St Mary's Churchyard footpath in Garston, possibly on a flat area just behind the garden of no.6 St Mary's Close, but by the 1920s it was down to just its lower walls and foundations. By the 1940s it was overgrown but still discernible, but in the 1950s workers from Manor Farm broke up the ground and cereal crops were planted, removing all trace of the barn. By this time the land was owned by the War Department and controlled by Durrington Land Agents.

The Manor: The Manor and Glebe Farm appear to have been farmed in tandem for many years. In the 18th century the Sanders family were tenants of Norton Paulet, probably at the Manor, and of the church at Glebe Farm. The Wallis family continued this tradition.

During William Wallis' time, Walter Long purchased the farm from Paul Methuen. Later the Wallis family became brewers and maltsters, landlords of the local public house, The King's Head, and grew their own barley. A 1910 tax made malting uneconomic and from that time the family concentrated on farming. In 1919 Frederick Wallis bought The Manor from Walter Hume Long, and Glebe Farm from the church after the death of his son John, who had been the tenant of Glebe Farm before going to war.

Horses were kept in stables adjoining the barn nearest to the pub. Between the two barns is the old threshing yard where the travelling threshing machine was once set up. The smaller barns near Glebe House were used to store horse-drawn farm tools. Six men worked on the farm and sheep were kept. [180]

In recent times The Manor lands have been sold to the Harley family at Valley farm. Just 30 acres and the buildings remain.

Glebe Farm: Glebe Farm, as its name suggests, is on church-owned land. The field opposite The King's Head next to the meadows is known as Tithing Field. In years gone by parsons derived income three ways: from tithes: 10% of parish produce; dues: fees payable at major festivals or burial; and glebe: farmland that went with the job. In 1890 the tithe was worth £106 per year and the glebe £206 for the whole of Chitterne. Tithes were abolished in 1936. The church lands or glebe in St Mary included the water meadows and land either side of the Heytesbury Road.

Thomas Sanders was the tenant at Glebe Farm in 1800. In 1808 Rev John Batchelor, Vicar of Chitterne, and the Diocese of Sarum, exchanged some glebe land with Paul Cobb Methuen. One plot the vicar acquired from Lord Methuen later became the site of the new vicarage for Chitterne St Mary.

Sometimes the Wallis' farmed Glebe Farm themselves, sometimes a manager was brought in. George Parham is shown next door to Wallis, at Glebe Farm, on the 1841 census, but he is gone by 1851. Mark Wallis farmed here, and Don Wallis, brother of Victor Wallis, farmed the 100 acres with 3 men while his brother farmed The Manor.

After Don Wallis' death in 1952 the Wallis family sold Glebe Farm and the farmhouse became separated from the farmland, as Don Wallis's widow was still living in it. They sold the land to a Mr Giles, of the 'Farmer Giles of Teffont' family, for his daughter Julie and her husband, Francis Crossman, to farm. The Crossmans were there 10 years and lived in no.105, one of the Glebe Farm Cottages. For the following 20 years or so the farm was managed by a succession of managers.

In 1982 Giles's grandson, Mark Lockyer moved into no.105 with his wife, Fiona, to run the farm. They introduced sheep to the beef cattle and arable regime and had a new farmhouse built alongside no.105. Today Glebe Farm is arable and the land is farmed from the Lockyer family farm at Dinton; Glebe Farmhouse and farm cottages were sold in 2001.

Clump Farm and Clump Farm Bridge c.1910

Clump Farm: Believed to be Biggs' farm. Paul Methuen bought Biggs' Farm in 1798. Samuel Biggs was bankrupt earlier and died in 1793. Samuel Biggs junior married Mary Hayward, daughter of Richard Hayward of Beechingstoke, 5 November 1776, with her father's consent. In the following century Richard Hayward's descendant bought Chitterne House, Gate House and accompanying farm in Chitterne All Saints.

John Veal leased Clump Farm in 1802, from Paul Cobb Methuen, for 99 years for lives of John Veal, Elijah Feltham, Joseph Compton and John Abery.[181] In 1851 the Lavington family farmed 674 acres. About 1870 Charles and Sarah Burbidge from Dorset farmed 490 acres, they employed 14 labourers and 4 boys, until at least 1890.[182] The Bazell family were at Clump Farm in 1901, and the Robinson family followed them. Harold Robinson died in the 1914-18 war and has a memorial in St Mary's graveyard. By 1927 William Webster farmed Clump Farm.[183]

The Websters delivered milk around the village from their dairy in a building where the Old Malthouse garages once stood.[184] Cows came down to the milking parlour on the path from the Clump and returned to the hill again after being milked. Winifred Webster married Victor Wallis of The Manor.

In 1935 the Strattons, farmers at Codford, bought the farm and put in a manager. The Garland family managed for the Strattons in 1937. They had pigs and cows.[185] Bacon and hams were stored in the barley waste in a shed close to the road in what is now Old Malthouse yard. Strattons water pump was in a shed between Meadow Cottage and Antoc. It fed Bridge Cottage as well as Clump Farm; the pipe was embedded in the structure of the bridge and froze for several weeks in winter 1962-63.[186] The house and pig farm were sold in the 1970s but the Strattons kept the land. They moved the dairy into a new unit called Chitterne Dairy on the Clump, with access from Shrewton Hill and Codford Road. The Oliver family bought Clump House and developers bought the pig farm and built St Mary's Close c1975. Redundant buildings at Chitterne Dairy have since been put to commercial use.

Valley Farm was created by the Harley family of Cheverell from 430 acres of The Manor land in Chitterne that they acquired. Valley Farmhouse, to house Jack Harley's family, and a barn were built on the new site.

In 1994 Jack Harley obtained a 10-year licence to use a dry valley on the farm as a landfill site, with access from the B390. Aberdeen Angus cross beef cattle are raised for the organic meat market and game birds are bred for shooting. In 2003 permission was given for a large shed to be built to finish organic beef cattle, this was erected in Spring 2004.

We can see now how entrepreneur farmers have learned to diversify as well as consolidate. At the western end of Chitterne farmland has been used for a landfill site. Redundant farm buildings at Chitterne Dairy house a computer firm, a close of houses has been built on a former pig farm and farmhouses have been sold to commuters who prefer to live in the country and work elsewhere. Completing the circle, sheep were reintroduced at Glebe Farm in the 1980s, but for their wool and meat this time. While at Valley Farm beef cattle are raised organically, to meet the growing demand by consumers following the Foot and Mouth, BSE crises and the GM debate. Game birds reared for sport are more numerous than rooks these days. Farming is suddenly front page news and everyone has an opinion. It is with growing interest that we watch to see where it goes from here.

Earning a Living

CHITTERNE 750 years ago was a busy, thriving, small town with regular markets and an annual fair that attracted traders from as far away as Old Sarum. The fair and markets brought the nuns much revenue and boosted Chitterne's status as a place to trade. This continued for hundreds of years; Pepys called Chitterne a town in 1668; it was still the biggest and most important place in the area until the 19th century. Then slowly, with the decline in revenue from farming, as its population and importance diminished, Chitterne was overtaken by neighbouring Shrewton. It's an astonishing thought that there was more going on in Chitterne in the Middle Ages when travel was difficult, than there is today when we can travel with such ease. Now for the most part we travel away from the village, we work, shop and find entertainment elsewhere, which has led to the demise of most village services.

Even 50 years ago Chitterne was a much busier place than it is today. In those days besides the eight farms in the village, there was a racing stable, two building companies, a carpenter/undertaker, a blacksmiths, a cycle repairer, a Ministry of Defence maintenance depot, two public houses, a guesthouse and two shops. While two bakers, two butchers, a greengrocer, a fish merchant, a hardware merchant, a laundryman and a milkman came and delivered around the village.[187] The change that has come about in village trades and services since the 1950s almost matches the change in farming. Now, in 2007, we have a carpenter, a welder and one public house, and only the milkman, laundryman and ice cream man remain of the regular deliverymen. But there are a few more homeworkers and sole traders in Chitterne nowadays. However, they tend not to trade with, or serve the villagers, but distant customers.

People who ran the village businesses 50 years and more ago needed to be adaptable, self-sufficient and mutually supportive. Self-sufficiency is no longer a priority, but mutual support and adaptability are still very much a part of modern Chitterne. For instance, delivering the mail to an isolated and widespread village like Chitterne required special arrangements. In 1859 the postman brought the Chitterne and Imber post from Codford by bicycle to Chitterne; at that time the village address was Chitterne, Codford. From Chitterne he continued on foot to Imber, where he spent his day doing odd jobs, before taking the afternoon mail back with him to Codford.[188]

The regular postman and his bicycle could not reach the outlying field barn cottages, so their post was delivered on foot. The field barn postman in the 1920s was retired Chitterne House gardener, Reginald Billet. Collecting his bundle of post from Mr Maidment's shop in Bidden Lane his circular route headed first for New Barn, then Two Barns, Bush Barn, Breach Hill, Bee Cottage, Down Barn and Penning Barn, a total of about 8 miles if there was mail for every settlement. As the field barn cottages gradually became unoccupied after World War 1 the route shortened but New House Farm and Middle Barn Cottages were added.[189] Later postal deliveries were made throughout the village by van.

Elizabeth Stokes was born to a family of agricultural workers in Bidden Lane in 1874, but because she could read and write fairly well, she broke with family tradition and worked at the Post Office at 53 Bidden Lane. The postmistress, Mrs Sarah Brown, wife of the schoolmaster, herself delivered the letters to the 'grand houses' on her bicycle, whereas Elizabeth carried villagers' letters in a basket and delivered them on foot. As most of the villagers were unable to read, she read the letters out loud for them in their homes. One time when the postmistress had an accident and could no longer ride her bicycle, Elizabeth was promoted to delivering to the houses of the gentry. At one house in particular, the 'Big House', an old lady whose sight was failing took a shine to Elizabeth and asked her to come and read the Sunday newspaper to her as well as the letters. Elizabeth loved these visits, as it was the first time she had ever walked on a real carpet, and she vowed one day she would have carpets herself.[190]

Frank Maidment, the Baptist preacher, succeeded Sarah Brown as postmaster in 1907. The Post Office was moved to his shop at 93 Bidden Lane where Frank also baked bread in his bakehouse near the shop.

His shop boasted a bell which gave off a sharp DING as you opened the door. To the left was the Post Office hatch, in front was the shop counter, and to the right was a large window-shelf to display goods. A large beam ran across the ceiling above the counter, on this were hung pairs of hob-nailed boots of all sizes, boot straps, card of studs and boot-tips (even small boys wore hob-nailed boots in those days). On the side of the counter were large blocks of carbolic and Sunlight 'washing' soap; I suppose that is why, when you opened the door you got a strong aroma of leather mixed with 'washing' soap.

The baking business carried on until the 1930s, but then Mr Maidment gave up baking and concentrated on the grocery shop and Post Office. He was always vigilant when behind his counter. If he discovered a member of his congregation trying to post off a bet on a favourite in a horse race, he would be ready to hold forth on 'the evils of gambling'. [191]

Following Frank Maidment's retirement as postmaster in 1949 the Post Office was moved to 65 Bidden Lane with Leonard Knock as postmaster. Still at number 65, Mrs Roberts succeeded Mr Knock. Mrs Roberts used the post office scales to weigh young babies as well as the post. After Mrs Roberts retired, John and Eileen Brown took over as postmasters and moved the Post Office to their general store at 17 Townsend. When the Browns retired to the old bakehouse next door at number 16 in 1974, Mr and Mrs Stevenson and Mrs Stevenson's brother Mr Purle took on the Post Office Stores. Mr Stevenson died in 1977, Mr Purle in 1998, and Mrs Stevenson retired in 2000. The building is now a private house and there is no post office or shop in the village, [192] the nearest is at Codford.

For many years Glebe Dairies at Codford, run by the Currie family, delivered milk to Chitterne. In the 1980s Glebe Dairies were taken over by King Street Dairies of Warminster and closed down; thereafter milk for Chitterne

Chitterne Post Office, Townsend in 1988.

was delivered from Warminster. Then King Street Dairies became Owens Dairy and later Planks Dairy. Bob Carter was the Chitterne milkman. He worked for all four dairy owners during his 45 years of delivering to Chitterne. In his early days at Codford, after delivering in our village, Bob returned to the dairy to make up the bottles of milk for the schoolchildren's afternoon break, filling each bottle by hand from a jug.

The natural resources for exploitation that Chitterne has in abundance, apart from farmland, are water, chalk and flint. Water has only comparatively recently been exported to other communities, we will come to that later. Chalk and flint have long been used locally in building, from lowly cob walls to knapped flint decorations for more grand houses. We will be looking at the building trade later too, but there is another resource within the parish, largely forgotten in modern times: clay.

This might sound as if I am contradicting myself having already stated that Chitterne lies on the chalk, but this is unusual geology. There is an extraordinary ridge of fine white clay intermingled with smooth round pebbles, which lies on top of the chalk of Chitterne St Mary Down.[193] By the 17th century someone, perhaps members of the Gauntlet family,[194] had found it to be the most perfect clay in England for making clay tobacco pipes.

Edward Fripp and Christopher Merewether were brothers-in-law and entrepreneurs. They took advantage of this new use for the clay and in 1651 acquired a licence for one year from Henry Paulet, Lord of the Manor of Chitterne St Mary, to dig 30 loads of it and cart it 9 miles east to Amesbury,[195] where the Gauntlets manufactured their famous clay pipes. Gauntlet pipes were considered the best 'for shape and colour' by Fuller and were praised by Ben Johnson.[196]

There were members of a Gauntlet family living in Chitterne in 1637; Phillip Gauntlet of Chitterne All Saints and Jonathan Gauntlet are mentioned.[197] William Pryor of Chitterne St Mary was a tobacco pipe maker.[198] The pits that resulted from the clay digging are still visible amongst a shroud of trees on Clay Pit Hill, on private land.

Carters and Carriers have been a necessity in this isolated village for time immemorial, whether carrying clay or goods or people. In the second half of the 19th century James George[199] and John Smith[200] were carriers in Chitterne All Saints. The George family ran a regular service to Warminster, possibly from The White Hart in Chitterne St Mary, picking up and dropping at the Anchor Hotel in Warminster Market Place.[201]

The White Hart Inn c.1940.

The White Hart has been a base for a carrier service probably from before Samuel Pepys' time, and later became the sole carrier in the village. By 1880 William Poolman was the carrier and innkeeper there.[202] In 1914 an unknown carrier started a motor carrier van service from Chitterne to Salisbury via Codford, but it must have been an uncomfortable ride as the van had solid tyres and carried livestock and deadstock as well as passengers.[203] Perhaps the unknown carrier was George Livings who was proprietor of the White Hart in 1921. Tragically his wife Amelia died that year leaving him with two little children.[204]

In the 1950s John Withers ran a bus from Bridge Cottage before moving to The White Hart. He sold up just two years later to Card's of Devizes who bought the bus business and the inn from him in 1957. They employed Maurice Newton to manage the carrier business; he died in 1977. After the Newtons left there was no carrier based in Chitterne. Boreham Coaches came out to the village from Warminster.[205]

Early carriers depended on the skills of the wheelwrights and farriers to keep their vehicles and horses in fine fettle. In Chitterne All Saints George and James Abery were carpenters and wheelwrights at Flint House[206] before Polden and Feltham. The Polden and Feltham firm of wheelwrights, carpenters and farriers was started in 1878 by brothers-in-law Clement Polden, son of Abdon, and William James Cockrell (Jimmy) Feltham.

Shoeing mules at Polden & Felthams in 1915.

Abdon Polden started a dynasty of builders and carpenters that continues to this day. As a young man he was mason in charge of the workmen building the new church in 1861. He spawned two businesses, Polden and Feltham and Polden Brothers. These two businesses worked so closely together that it was difficult to distinguish them. When constructing a house Polden Brothers built the walls and Polden and Feltham provided the carpentry. For a large job they would pool all their resources.

First, Polden and Feltham: Jimmy Feltham was married to Clement's sister, Alma Charlesanna. Clement Polden lived at Flint House and Jimmy and Alma lived at number 98 on the Codford Road. In the yard at Flint House there was a double forge, a smithy, a carpenter's shop, a paint and plumber's shop and a timber shed with deep sawing pits.[207]

This was a real family business; Alf Burt, the blacksmith often worked with Clement and Jimmy, repairing traction engines and bonding wagon wheels. Alf was married to another of Abdon Polden's daughters, Florence. Geoff Feltham, Frank Polden and Percy Feltham worked for them too, and of course Clement's two sons Alban and Owen Polden eventually took over the business from their father and uncle and ran it until 1972, almost reaching the firm's centenary.

Now we come to the building Poldens, but before we look at them more closely I want to briefly tell of the humble cob wall. The grander old houses in the village are built of stone and flint or brick. There was no stone or brick available locally, only flint and chalk, which were the two basic building commodities used for humbler

Alban and Owen Polden bonding a wheel at Polden &
Felthams c.1960s.

dwellings in the old days. When mixed with other local by-products of the farming industry they could be used to build a 'cob' wall. This type of wall was common in Chitterne in past times. Provided its 'head' and 'feet' were kept dry, 'a good hat and a good pair of boots' as old countrymen would say, a cob wall would last for many years. The old village school was constructed in this way and there are still a few remaining sections of cob garden walls to be seen in the village.

Thomas George, 1750-1820, was a cob wall builder. He lived in Chitterne All Saints all his life and there follows his recipe for constructing a cob wall.

How to build a Cob Wall[208]

Dig a foundation trench 20 inches wide by 24 inches deep. Fill it to ground level with flint stones, grouted together with a mixture of mashed chalk, chaff and water.

Make the shuttering by driving elm posts, 6 foot long, 3' by 3', into the ground at the sides of the trench and brace them at regular intervals, enough to support wide elm boards. Tie the elm boards to the posts. No more than 15 feet in length, and half the finished height to be boarded at once.

Fetch soft chalk in ox-carts from the chalk pit. Break it up to a workable consistency and mix with measured amounts of chaff, cut-straw, cow and horse hair, or sheep wool, water and fine grit, collected from the road-sides, to a not too sloppy, sticky mortar.

Shovel the resulting mix into the shuttering. Insert an upright keying post in the stop-end, to key in to the next section of wall.

Tread the mixture down with bare feet and tamp it with a rammer. Add soft stone and clean rubble to fill the middle.

When halfway built, add the top shutter-boards and tie in place. Continue to build as before.

When the finished height is reached, shape a pointed ridge along the top and bed in it elm tie-rails 2 x 1½ inches, two each side, and wire them into the soft mortar. Being sure to scoop out handfuls of mortar under the rails at regular intervals to allow for the under-thatch to be tied in place.

After drying-out thatch the wall. Anchor the thatch with withy spars, tamp it lightly and trim.

Polden Brothers, builders, were Arthur Polden's three sons, Ernie, Eric and Gerald Polden. Arthur was Abdon's cousin, he and his son Ernie

Cob walls in Pitt's Lane.

lived in the Poplars, which Arthur had renovated from an old Blacksmith's workshop. Eric and Gerald lived at numbers 58 and 59 Bidden Lane. Polden Brothers yard was in Back Lane behind the Poplars. Arthur's nephew, Cecil Windsor, worked for Polden Bros. as a mason. When grit for render was scarce they collected grit from the roadsides to use instead and washed it on the village green in large tubs of water from the Cut.

The brothers worked for John Wallis Titt on many of his installations, including the windpump at Spot's Pool, where they were responsible for concreting the feet firmly into the ground, and a series of four windpumps that worked together to raise water to the top of a hill on the Bapton Manor estate. They even travelled as far as France; Cecil Windsor went to France with them when they erected windpumps there.

The company was also responsible for building Syringa Cottage for Bill Brown, the Metropolitan Police detective, when he retired to Chitterne. Bill Windsor, great grandson of Abdon Polden, started out working for Polden Brothers. Then, about 40 years ago, he began his own one-man building concern, employing contract carpenters and plasterers as needed. John Brown, the carpenter from 16 Townsend, often worked with Bill. Now, in 2007, Bill's son Nick Windsor, a carpenter by trade, carries on the family tradition, he has his own one-man outfit producing high-class joinery.[209]

Alfred Burt, the blacksmith, was a busy man when Chitterne Racing Stables were in full swing. He shod all R.J.Farquharson's racehorses at Chitterne and at Tilshead too. Ronald James Farquharson bought a sporting establishment in Chitterne in 1906 when he returned to England after a successful career in Ceylon as a tea and rubber planter. Farquharson had ridden horses as an amateur in Ceylon and India and chose Wiltshire as his base for a new venture as racehorse owner and trainer. He also acquired Chitterne Lodge and Tilshead Lodge for his training and stud farm purposes, as well as Chitterne Farm and 3000 acres of farmland. Chitterne Lodge had been used as a farmhouse before the decline in farming; Tilshead Lodge had been an equestrian establishment since at least the 17th century when the King's horses were stabled there.

At Chitterne Farquharson probably had the block of stables built and used Lodge Cottage to house his stable lads. He installed his racing stables manager in Chitterne Lodge. In the 1920s this was a Mr G Clancy, who had not only winning horses but also a winning man in his employ. In 1927, Ernie Stanter, one of his young stablemen won the stable lads' flat race at a sports meeting arranged for jockeys and stablemen at Doncaster Races. Princess Mary presented Ernie with his prize of 35 shillings, shook his hand and congratulated him.[210]

Gentle Shepherd was probably the most famous of Farquharson's horses, but he never raced. As a stud horse at Tilshead he sired a few winners, including Shepherdess. Shepherdess' winning descendants were Truckle, Rural Lass, Combined Operations, Clover Bud and Go Ballistic. Farquharson's greatest racing success was with Mount William, winner of the Irish Derby and Wokingham Handicap. Ronald James Farquharson died in 1934.[211]

Jim and Mary Ford bought Chitterne Lodge and the Stables from the War Department in the early 1950s. Jim ran the Racing Stables, and his wife Mary ran the Lodge as a Guest House.

Jim's most notable success was with Gay Donald the winner of the Cheltenham Gold cup in 1955. Gay Donald was ridden by jockey Tony Grantham and owned by the Burts, a farming family from Sutton Veny. He was a very friendly and idiosyncratic horse who loved Liquorice Allsorts and tucking into Jim's sardine sandwiches on an awayday. For many years one of the horseshoes from his huge feet was displayed on a beam at the village pub, The King's Head.[212]

Jim had many other wins and was a popular trainer in racing circles. He is remembered through the Jim Ford Chase held at Wincanton every year, and the Jim Ford Cup, the winner's cup that he and Mary donated. Sadly, Jim died in 1970, and the Racing Stables were sold to Ian Dudgeon. Ian carried on training horses for many years and had an all-weather track constructed behind Paddock House, before selling the stables to developers.

As motor power replaced horsepower, a different type of repairer was needed. In the 1920s Frank Sheppard did not repair motor vehicles, but he did repair bicycles, clocks, watches and other mechanical devices, as well as re-charging accumulators. He ran the business from his home at Pitt's House and he was possibly one of the first people in the village to own a car, an Austin 7.[213]

The first motor vehicle repair business in the village grew out of John Withers' abandoned business at Bridge Cottage that included a café, coach business and a petrol pump. Henry Slater and Lily Poolman had opened Bridge Café in a single storey extension behind Bridge Cottage during World War II, to cater for the needs of the many troops who were training on the Plain. When Graham and Linda Dean bought Bridge Cottage from John Withers in 1955, they paid £2250 with a loan from the Cleveland Petrol Company for their first business venture. They started

Bridge Café c.1940s.

Graham Dean in 1994 with the three-wheeler van he renovated in Chitterne.

trading at Bridge Cottage on 7th December, and took £2.7s.4½d., selling 36½ gallons of petrol that first week.

The enterprise was hard work as the premises were ramshackle and the services dire when they moved in. Nevertheless despite the drawbacks Linda and Graham ran the café, a bed and breakfast business, one petrol pump, two self-drive hire cars, a vehicle repair shop and charged accumulators for radios.

In 1956 the Suez crisis and petrol rationing threatened the Deans livelihood, but undeterred and with true entrepreneurial spirit Graham branched out into mink breeding. The trend of farming mink in back gardens for the fur trade was sweeping the nation at the time and Graham thought he would have a go as mink pelts could fetch £30 each. He started with six mink, kept in cages, and fed on scraps collected from various food businesses in the locality. The six mink became one hundred. Sometimes the mink escaped into the grounds of The King's Head next door and Graham would tempt them back with a handful of raw liver. Once Graham's two occupations collided: he was chasing a fugitive mink with a handful of gory liver when he startled a motorcyclist waiting at the pumps to be served. The motorcyclist was more than a little dismayed by the sight of the petrol attendant's hand covered in blood, as Graham gave a hasty explanation and dashed off to complete his quest. Not a scene a customer expected to find in the normally quiet village of Chitterne.

Apart from the petrol rationing and mink breeding phase things went well at Bridge Cottage and Garage. A second petrol pump, a new garage building and a little kiosk selling cigarettes and sweets at the side of the cottage were added. The Deans were a welcome addition to the village as Graham had skills and equipment that were useful in a crisis. He once helped Francis Crossman of Glebe Farm free a cow that had its head jammed between some bars. It was a dark, snowy winter's night when Graham got the call. He loaded his oxyacetylene welding gear and cutters in the farmer's pick-up and, towing his gas bottles behind, they drove across the snow-covered field to reach the stricken cow. Using the pick-up headlights in order to see, Graham cut through the metal bars while Francis tried to hold the animal steady. They succeeded and the cow was none the worse for its ordeal.

Later the Deans gave up the café and concentrated on the bed and breakfast, garage and petrol businesses. In 1971, with a growing family, they moved away from Chitterne. Graham continued running the garage business but let out the cottage and petrol pumps to a series of tenants. The petrol pumps were removed when they no longer conformed to new government regulations, and Graham and Linda sold Bridge Cottage in 1996. Graham Dean retired in 2000 and closed his

The King's Head and Bridge Garage in the 1970s.

garage business after 45 years of trading in Chitterne.

The long-suffering landlord of The King's Head at the time of the Deans mink breeding exploits was Cecil Newton. Cecil and Doris Newton ran The King's Head for many years until the untimely death of Cecil in 1980. By then it was the only public house in the village, The White Hart hav- ing been declared redundant and closed in the 1960s after more than 300 years of trad- ing. We have touched on the carrier busi- ness at The White Hart earlier, which was part of the inn's service from early days. Whereas The King's Head had stables for 11 horses but no carrier service; it was how- ever home to a public weighbridge, which was sited in front of the pub. Publicans at The King's Head in the 19th century were

Drilling for water alongside the Tilshead road in 1985.

described as both 'landlord and surveyor'.[214] In those days the Wallis family pro- vided the beer for the community. They not only leased the pub, and were land- lords, but brewed beer in the pub's brewhouse, using the malt they had made from their own barley, grown in their own fields in Chitterne. At the beginning of the 20th century a tax on malting made the process uneconomic and put an end to that endeavour. The pub was sold to a brewery at about the same time, and was owned by Ushers and later by Gibbs Mew.[215] Gibbs Mew sold The King's Head in 2002 and it remains privately owned today.

Lastly we come to water, which we have looked at briefly earlier. It is the third commodity in copious supply in the village. Chitterne water has only recently been exploited for use by folk other than the residents of the village. In 1974 the newly formed Wessex Water Authority was granted the licence to extract water from the Upper Wylye Valley at Chitterne. Seven boreholes were made alongside the Tilshead Road and a new pumping station was constructed nearby in 1986. Chitterne water was first supplied in 1988, destined for the residents of Trowbridge and other growth areas of West Wiltshire, as well as Chitterne village. The boreholes are around 70

Wessex Water's Chitterne Pumping Station.

metres deep and 90 cm across and the maximum rate of abstraction is 20 million litres per day. The new award winning automatically controlled pumping station is monitored at the Regional Control Room at Bath. The water is pumped to a new reservoir at Strawberry Hill, West Lavington and is said to be naturally of a very high quality, low in nitrates and containing no trace of pesticides.[216] In subsequent years the extraction of water caused serious depletion of the volume of water in the Chitterne Brook, this was remedied by adding water to the brook on the southern side of the village; a sort of water by-pass.

The Military Effect

They own the parish of Imber and will soon have acquired the whole parish of
Chitterne. The Times, December 1930.

W HATEVER FEELINGS were prevalent at the time amongst the villagers
when the War Department first started buying land for troop training on
the Plain, nowadays the relationship with the Ministry of Defence is very good.
Over the last 20 years the MoD has made significant efforts to minimise the effects
of military exercises for the inhabitants of the Plain and to promote the advantages
of MoD ownership of the chalk upland, backed up by archaeologists.

Although the War Department had been purchasing land on the Salisbury
Plain since 1897, before World War I they did not own any in Chitterne. But that is
not to say that their presence was not felt in the village. Writing soon after the end
of hostilities, and still raw from the task of ministering to bereaved families, Rev.
J.T. Canner, vicar of Chitterne during WWI, had this to say of the effects of the
Great War on Chitterne:

> . . . history treats the rank and file who do the actual fighting in war very ill. It commonly
> forgets all about them. These following facts have been put together that they may
> not be forgotten. A soldier's life in actual wartime has its hardships, its excitements,
> its miraculous escapes, its exultation and despair. They toil in the burning sun, they
> suffer in the rain sodden trenches, they experience the biting frosts, when a man
> walking a few yards with his tin of water finds it frozen by the time he reaches his
> dug-out, they grumble at their hard fate, but endure. All honour to them.
>
> With smokeless powder and long-range guns the soldier may not see the enemy
> he is fighting against, for days together yet the firing goes on, men are killed miles

and miles away from the point where the shell was sent on its journey of destruction. Men speak of a 'League of Nations' to prevent war, but if it is to be of any practical use, it must be backed by united force and ready to wield it if necessary. Words of wisdom may flow from the lips of the British Solomon, but they are valueless when unaccompanied by the glint of cold steel. The nations will pay no heed to an arbiter who is not clad in shining armour.

When tidings of the Great War were published, men were immediately forthcoming to assist in the terrible undertaking. Although there were no hutments erected in the parish, yet there were many within a few yards of the boundary and many men were billeted in the houses of the village.

Chitterne children's army in World War 1. Percy Churchill is sixth from right in the front row. In the background are from the left: Chitterne House; Pitt's Cottage and Pitt's House.

Even the children were greatly excited over the war and showed their military enthusiasm by parading the village. They even marched as far as the camps at Tilshead (4 miles) and the Scottish Highlanders were so pleased with this exhibition of loyalty that after giving them a good repast their Pipers accompanied the youthful enthusiasts back to our village.

A very important artillery range was constructed during the Great War and the shells coming from a distance of 6 to 13 miles fell in the parish. All kinds of experiments by night and day were tried there and officers had special observation posts erected in order to watch the effect of the shells upon the companie of dummy soldiers, wire entanglements and dugouts. American Generals also came here to gain knowledge before going out to the front. And King George considered it to be so important an experimental and training station that he paid a visit to the parish.

The villagers became quite accustomed to being aroused at 4 a.m. on Thursdays by the strains of the New Zealand Band. This Band accompanied as far as our village, men who had become convalescent again after their military troubles and were being marched to Sting Camp before being sent off again to the Front. It caused sad feelings in our hearts and many a prayer went up to the Almighty for their preservation.[217]

4th Battalion of the Wiltshire Regiment in Delhi, India, World War 1. Chitterne men in the back row: ? Poolman second from left and Lewis Feltham fourth. Front row: Geoffrey Feltham fourth from left and William Churchill fifth.

Over eighty men from Chitterne served in World War 1 and seven of its young men died. Five of them died in the last months of the conflict. They are commemorated on the village war memorial outside the Church and by the stained glass window inside donated by the Hayward family.

During the 1920s the War Department continued to buy large portions of land, but now in the vicinity of Chitterne. By 1930 they had acquired 20,000 acres of Salisbury Plain. Most significantly they had purchased the whole of the neighbouring parish of Imber. The anonymity of the area disappeared. For the Plain villages of Chitterne, Tilshead and Imber had been almost unknown to the general population before the purchases, but afterwards their names, and even maps showing their position, regularly appeared in the press. Every newspaper reader had heard of them.[218]

When farmers in the Warminster area were notified that the War Department still needed large stretches of land, it was thought they would soon acquire the whole of Chitterne. The Times newspaper quoted that there were 'serious complaints from archaeologists and agriculturalists.' And at the Warminster Urban Council meeting the Water Committee reported that 50,000 gallons of water were wanted by the military for 3 months.[219]

However, these initial fears that the entire parish of Chitterne would soon fall prey to military take-over as Imber had done, proved to be unfounded. Nevertheless, by 1937 the War Department had compulsorily purchased all of R.J. Farquharson's estates and land, amounting to 3000 acres, as well as Manor Farm and Elm Farm buildings and lands, and all the outlying field barn settlements. The three farms in the old Chitterne St Mary parish, The Manor, Clump Farm and Glebe Farm remained in private hands.

The land newly acquired by the War Department around Chitterne became part of the Western Range of the SPTA or Salisbury Plain Training Area, where troops practised tactics and firing. To the left of the road to Tilshead from Chitterne they would be firing live rounds and to the right, blanks. The live firing area, around Imber, was designated a danger area and the rights of way that crossed this area were cut off. Some tracks that had previously led to outlying cottages and field barns became overgrown with lack of use; army and farm vehicles used the rest.

The new landlords in Chitterne made some changes. They introduced three categories of land, Schedules 1, 2 and 3. Schedule 3 land was grassland that remained grassland. Schedule 2 was land that had been under the plough and was now converted to grass- *MoD sign marking schedule 1* land. Schedule 1 land was leased out by the War Depart- *land on Chitterne Farm west,* ment and could be ploughed. Farmers who leased this *formerly Manor Farm.*

Tank crossing 'L' on the Tilshead road.

land would be compensated if the military manoeuvres resulted in damage to the crops.

In the village itself farm cottages now owned by the WD were numbered separately from other village dwellings and local men were employed by the Defence Property Services Agency to look after them. The agency had a depot at the former farmyard of Elm Farm.

Where previously the village roads had been 'bad and exposed'[220] now the War Department strengthened some of them with concrete under the tarmac, for heavier army traffic. Road signs appeared alongside village roads warning of tanks, or later banning tanks from certain roads. Tank crossings, where tank tracks crossed roads, were marked by two rows of old railway sleepers topped by bright yellow caps. Some of these have recently been replaced by metal posts, but still with yellow caps.

During World War II a small number of soldiers were billeted in Chitterne, some of them at Chitterne Lodge, which had been acquired by the War Department as part of the late R.J. Farquharson's estate. Others, with families, lived in rented accommodation. The local schools accommodated both soldier's children and evacuees from London, who started arriving in the village about 1940 and were allocated to Chitterne families by retired police chief, Bill Brown. The Bridge Café was opened by Henry Slater to cater for the needs of troops in the area.

A group of Italian prisoners of war were brought to the village to work on the Cut. They deepened it and strengthened the inside of the bank on the road side by lining it with concrete blocks.

The Chitterne contingent of the Local Defence Volunteers or LDV was formed in the early 1940s. Their headquarters was an old shepherd's hut at the top of Shrewton Hill alongside the track to Yarnbury. The LDV, renamed the Home Guard in 1943/44, were commanded by Mr Limbrick, who lived and farmed at Manor Farm. The Guard were occasionally joined on exercise by a group of Army Cadets who lived in the village, but were based in Codford.

Chitterne Home Guard and Army Cadets outside Manor Farmhouse during World War II. Back row left to right: ? (Starchy) Burton; Geoff Helps; John Patterson; Bert Bailey; Bert Diaper; Leslie Sheppard; George Gagen; Ernie Polden. Second row: Les Mundy; Walt Herrington; Walt Ledbury; George Dowdell; John Lecocq (Channel Islands); unknown; Don Wallis; Will Ashley, Alban Polden; Len Moore; Herbie Feltham; Bert Lush; Mr Fagg. Third row: Fred Bowden; Rowland Pearce; Jack Beaumont; Douglas Piercy; Bert Diaper; Dickie Bailey; George Macey; 'Pat' Patterson; ? (Chirpy) Grant; Willie Ashley; William Poolman; Fred Feltham; Stan Waite; Frank Helps; Lewis Feltham; Frank Ashley. Fourth row: Len Searchfield; Harry Sheppard; Percy Churchill; Cecil Windsor; Louis Daniels; Sgt. Blatch (Codford); unknown (Heytesbury); Mr Limbrick (Leader); Tom Limbrick; ? (Snobby) Snelgrove (Codford); Evelyn Feltham; Jack Poolman; unknown (number 2); Bill Bartlett. In the front row are the infamous Chitterne cadets whose exploits would have made a good episode of Dad's Army: Cecil Saxby; Laurence Wallis; John George; Tony Bailey; Gerald Feltham; George Feltham; Billy Windsor; John (Chippy) Oakes; Gerald Polden; Bobby Gorry.

It was decided that it would be a good idea for the newly formed guard to practise apprehending the enemy, in case of a future invasion. So the Chitterne cadets were given the task of pretending to be 'Germans.' They were told to go and hide in the village. The guard were to seek them out and apprehend them. But, so successful were the cadets at performing their roles in the exercise, that not one single 'German' was caught.

Later, the very disgruntled and embarrassed Home Guard accused the cadets of cheating by hiding in trees. The crafty cadets had won the day by using their local knowledge. Some hid inside old hollow trees and others climbed up into the lime trees that bordered the Walk well out of sight of their elders.[221]

As well as a Home Guard, Chitterne had at least two Air Raid Wardens, William Churchill[222] and Thomas Gorry,[223] were appointed. At the first sign of an air raid it was their job to cycle from one end of the village to the other blowing a trumpet.

At the first air raid this was done perfectly, except that whoever was on duty forgot to sound the all clear later. So, technically, Chitterne is still under curfew.

The village was very nearly bombed one Saturday night when a dance was in progress at the Village Hut. A German bomber dropped 21 bombs. The first one landed in the first big field on the left going towards Codford, the rest were dropped in an arc with the last one just missing the road to Warminster. One young girl at the dance was so scared that she fainted right away and had to be revived.

William Churchill's Air Raid Warden's Warrant Card.

Two drawings of how Chitterne Barn might have looked in its heyday.

Some village lads had a narrow escape from enemy guns when they were gathering piles of straw with a horse and trailer in farmer Robert Long's fields. A Heinkel III German plane suddenly flew in low with it's machine-guns firing directly at them. Luckily no one was hit. At the time the Poldens had just had a shiny new roof put on their field shed and this was blamed for attracting the pilot. One of the bullets went clean through a pigsty and a pig's trough, the head of the bullet lodging in the opposite side of the trough, letting all the water out. The pilot was clearly seen by other village lads from their window in The Round House, and they felt sure he saw them too as he swooped to avoid the large chestnut tree in their garden. They were sure he would have fired at them save for his need to clear the tree.[224] The plane was later shot down near New Zealand Farm at Gore Cross.

Young boys of the village were fascinated by military finds and took extraordinary risks. A group of them headed for Breakheart Bottom when Blenheim bombers were firing 20mm cannon guns and dropping bombs on the bombing range. They stayed out of range during firing and bombing, then dashed out between rounds to fill a sack with propeller blades from the bombs. Some young village lads, all brothers, found an unexploded 5 cwt US skid bomb that they rolled to a well and dropped over the side. Luckily for them it failed to explode. Others collected American plastic explosive and used it to blow up a tree at Fox Covert. Pieces of the tree fell up to 150 yards away.[225]

During the war the BBC made recordings of various British dialects to be sent to the troops stationed abroad as reminders of home. William Poolman of Chitterne was chosen to represent the West Country dialect.

Two men of Chitterne lost their lives in World War II: Lieutenant Edwin George of the Wiltshire Regiment and Private Leonard Salter of the Green Howards.

After the war the War Department sometimes made decisions regarding village property that were viewed as plain daft. Before 1951 they refused to allow a piped supply of water to be installed to the council houses where water was still being hand-drawn;[226] in 1955, when houses owned by the WD in the village were vacant, the Land Agent intended to let them to farmers from outside the area, when there were villagers who were without a roof over their heads. But common sense prevailed and they were let to the villagers who were homeless. However, some years later when the WD, now the Ministry of Defence, made a sensible suggestion concerning Chitterne Barn, they were thwarted.

Since acquiring it in the 1930s, the army had been using Chitterne Barn as a briefing shelter. The thatched roof had long since rotted away and been covered by sheets of corrugated tin, but the oak supports that had stood for over 200 years were still good and worth preserving. So, in preparation for the proposed building of the new training village on Copehill Down, it was decided to remove the barn to a safer environment.

Chitterne Barn was dismantled for the MoD by a Youth Training Scheme team from Bristol led by Colin Brain and Dave Richards. The team camped on the Plain in summer 1983 and painstakingly took the historic barn apart stone by stone and beam by beam. That was probably the easiest part; putting it back together in its new home provided 'a real challenge,' according to the team leaders. It was to be part of Hartcliffe Community Council's Park Farm in Bristol; a project to build a community farm staffed by New Deal youngsters, as well as regular staff and volunteers, that would be open to the public. The team succeeded in reassembling the barn, a great achievement, but without the thatch, as that would have proved too expensive, it was given a tiled roof and used for storing hay, sheltering animals and for lambing.

However, ten years later, on August 31st 1993, fate intervened and dealt the barn a cruel blow. For Chitterne Barn, that had been so carefully moved to spare it from army manoeuvres, became the target of a young arsonist and that night it was burnt to the ground. The offender, from an institution for disturbed children, who was known to have been suffering from pyromania, was later caught and dealt with.[227] Chitterne Barn is described in more detail in the Farming chapter.

FIBUA village on Copehill Down.

The training village, or FIBUA: Fighting In Built-Up Areas, was built in 1986 on Copehill Down against the wishes of the majority of the people of Chitterne. There were protests and meetings and villagers appeared on the TV news, but all to no avail. The villagers were told that a training village was needed to prepare troops for the possibility of a third world war that was expected to take place on the continent in Saxony. Thus the FIBUA village was to be built to resemble a village of that region, high on the open plain, at a rumoured cost of £10,000,000.

Despite the protests the planned building work went ahead and concrete houses soon sprouted up, where before there had been just the wild chalkland flora. Swathes

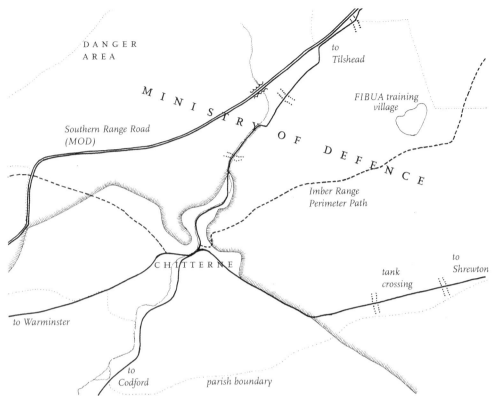

Map of Military Lands

of trees were planted in carefully planned groups in the surrounding area and rights of way were diverted around the new development. The villagers were worried that squatters or travellers might move into the empty buildings huddling around the taller replica church. But reassurances were given that there would be a continuous presence guarding the site, and slowly we became used to the FIBUA village and no longer stared at it as we drove past.

Only three years later the Berlin wall came down and the purported scenario for hostilities disappeared. The temptation for Chitterne people to say 'we told you so' was very strong, and many thought the MoD had created a white elephant. But since that time other threats have emerged, so the FIBUA village has been far from redundant. It has been adapted as necessary for training troops for fighting in Bosnia, and lately for Iraq.

One of the most common complaints regarding army movements in Chitterne, besides that of the noise and vibration of tanks going by, concerned the amount of mud deposited on the village roads by army vehicles. Partly to these ends the MoD built themselves the Southern Range Road. This is a road purely for army traffic that would connect all the camps on the south of the Salisbury Plain with Warminster, and eventually with Tidworth. The new road would also help preserve the natural life and history of the Plain, by keeping the army traffic to specific routes. Since the roads construction it has become a rare sight to see an armoured personnel carrier or tank in the village. And with the advent of mud-clearing vehicles, that appear when an exercise is on, our village roads are rarely covered in mud from army vehicles.

There must be something about the village that attracts army personnel. For, far from being deterred by our wild Plain weather during training, many ex-soldiers choose to spend their retirement in Chitterne.

MoD sign marking the Imber Range. In the distance are Down Barn trees; the Southern Range Road passes through Breakheart Bottom in front of the trees.

Beer and bandage race at the Royal wedding celebrations 1981.

Fun and Games

The Hall forms part of the heart of this community where people meet regularly for
a variety of activities.[228]

FOR PEOPLE LIVING in our small village on the Salisbury Plain in the past there was little chance to seek entertainment in the towns, unless you were one of the well off and owned a horse and trap. So entertainment had to be homegrown and provided locally. In this regard the villagers of 100 years ago seem to have been well catered for. There were football, cricket and tennis clubs, a village band, a village benefit club, two public houses, summer fetes, tea-parties, outings and celebrations, besides all the usual festivities associated with the farming year such as Harvest Festival, and those connected with the religious festivals of Easter and Christmas.

The Chitterne Brass Band was the catalyst for most of the village festivities, providing the music for many a fete, celebration and village folk dancing on the green. Folk dancing was once an old tradition in the village, especially on a summer evening after a Village Benefit Club feast at the school. One of the favourite dances in the late 19th century was 'Bricks and Mortar'. It was a vigorous dance that went on and on, exhausting the participants.[229] Some time during the following half-century folk dancing in Chitterne died out, except for the village children who were encouraged to join in the revival of country dancing that swept the country between the wars.

From at least as early as 1850 the greatest celebration of the year was the annual Band Fete held on Whit Monday in the Whitsuntide Field. The Whitsuntide Field was the former name of the present day Sportsfield. After the Mansion House was demolished, the cleared site was perfect for holding village gatherings. For the

Chitterne Band c1890. Bandmaster Abdon Polden in the centre and Mark Titt is behind him on the right.

first 100 years or so the ground was privately owned and permission had to be sought of the owner, the Onslows and then the Collinses. But later, when it was owned by the War Department, protracted negotiations by Mr Scott-Bolton of St Mary's Lodge to buy it for the village were finally successful, and the field became the property of the village and is managed by the parish council.

So Whit Monday was eagerly anticipated every year as the day of the Band Fete. There were swinging boats, Aunt Sally, coconut shies and maypole dancing in 1887. In 1904 Mr Dainton of the King's Head provided liquid refreshments; sweets and pastries were sold by Messrs Withy and Burgess in one of the tents that were scattered about the field and the ladies of the village served tea in the schoolroom at 4.30 p.m. with milk provided by the Misses Collins. Whilst in 1927, besides the usual favourites, there was skittling for a pig. And all the while the band played a selection of favourite tunes, except for an interval when the players had a break for a well-earned drink of beer.

Abdon Polden was bandmaster for many of those early years but after he died in 1924 the band's fortunes declined and by 1928 a special concert was held to try and revive interest and raise money for the band's coffers. This was successful and the band survived. In the 1930s they could be heard playing at Miss Awdry's garden fetes.

Miss Awdry opened her garden at The Grange for a fete every year in aid of her favourite charity. She was fond of local children and encouraged them to come along and perform country dances in front of the band. Arthur Scott, her gardener, was none too pleased about all the young feet damaging his flowerbeds, but Miss Awdry held sway. The treasure hunt was a highlight of the occasion for the paying fete guests. Numbered labels were secreted amongst the plants and shrubs, but within reach of the paths, and small boys avidly sought to be the first to find them and point them out, trampling the plants in the process. Beside the hunt there were skittles, hoop-la, coconut shies and Aunt Sally on the main lawn, the Chitterne Brass Band playing soft music to one side and tea tables the other, while Mrs Scott, the Grange cook, served great dollops of yellow ice cream from the kitchen window.[230]

From 1840 indoor village entertainment was held at the school, which had been built as a base for the Village Benefit Club as well as for learning. An alternative venue was the Penny Reading Room, but this was very small and unsuitable for activities for the whole village. The Penny Reading Room was still being supported

Miss Collins' tea party at Manor Farm early 1900's. Chitterne Band members are behind the children in the centre.

in 1901, by money raising concerts in the schoolroom of instrumental and vocal music, compered by the Rev. Sylvester.[231]

After World War 1 an opportunity arose for the village to purchase one of the many redundant army huts. A parish meeting approved this suggestion, and formed a Village Hut Committee, after deciding that current facilities at the school were no longer convenient for village events. When an ex-army stores hut became available it was purchased by public subscription and in 1920–21 Polden & Feltham dismantled and re-assembled it on land in Bidden Lane donated by Jimmy Feltham. The Hut had a main hall with a raised platform at The White Hart end, a clubroom heated by a tortoise stove and a small room. It was used for meetings, whist drives, dances, parties for children and the elderly, and other events that were held in the daytime when the school was unavailable. The humble building soon became an essential part of village life and a Village Hut Club came into being. Older villagers nearly always speak of the Hut with affection, for their families had all contributed towards it and enjoyed themselves there.

Cricket in fancy dress? c.1925. Standing from left: Fred Feltham; unknown; Collenso Bailey; Lewis Feltham; unknown; Stan Feltham; unknown; unknown; unknown; Mrs Nottage. Sitting: unknown; Nora Feltham; Beryl Feltham; Esme Feltham; the rest are unknown.

The Village Hut Club put on concerts in the Hut, including solos, monologues, sketches and a finale to raise money for club funds. These entertainments were very successful, and thoroughly enjoyed by the large audiences. During World War

II dances were held at the hut and soldiers stationed nearby joined the revelry on Saturday nights. A blind pianist from Westbury played the Hut piano, assisted by his wife. After the war a group of local musicians played together at dances. Three of the Le Cocq sisters, Margaret, Harriet and Nicola played the piano and accordion in turn accompanied by either Bill Windsor or Bobby Gorry on the drums. In the breaks Mr Fagg played records.[232]

Village youths who wanted to make their own fun got up to all sorts of pranks outside the Hut and around The White Hart alehouse at the bottom of the Lane. As ever the older people of the village were annoyed by this and constantly berated the youngsters in an effort to disperse them.[233] Jimmy Feltham, always one to encourage discipline in village youngsters, started the Young Men's Club and ran it until the start of World War II. It was held in the Hut every day except Sunday; village youths could play billiards for 2d. a game, or darts. Some of the young men put on entertainments in the Hut in aid of their club. They called themselves the Sparks Concert Party; two of Jimmy Feltham's daughters, Esme and Nora, rehearsed them and Miss Burt played the piano.

In the mid 1940s former club members, Eric Polden and Eddie Poolman, took over as leaders, assisted by some of the responsible older lads.[234] Younger village boys were encouraged to join the 1st Chitterne Wolf Cubs. Rev. Biddlecombe, a keen scout himself, led the pack in the 1950s. In later years a Youth Club, for both girls and boys, was held in the village. Fred and Kathleen Babey were leaders when the Youth Club members raised the greatest portion of the cost of the sports field.

The Mothers' Union held a Christmas Party for the village children in the Hut. The Father Christmas stood under the Christmas tree, which was perfect, just how you would imagine the tree should be, and he gave every child a Christmas present. Various village gentlemen played Father Christmas; Alf Burt was a regular. One year it was Rev. Yeomans, the vicar, but his daughter Alison discovered his identity when she recognised her father's wellies.[235] All these entertainments moved to the school building when the school closed in the 1960s. The Hut had had its day, and closed its doors for the last time after almost 50 years, and a new era began. The school was refurbished and re-opened in 1970 as the new Village Hall.

In the 1960s an annual favourite was the village garden show. Great bucketfuls of colourful dahlias were for sale and the competition for the funniest shaped vegetable was hotly contested. The entries caused much amusement, especially twin carrots or carrots shaped like noses.[236] There was always fierce competition among the gardeners to produce the best of each kind of vegetable. Garden shows are not held today. There are fewer homegrown vegetables and most of the former allotments have disappeared, although as I write early in 2007 there is talk of renewed interest in the latter.

The annual village fete and gymkhana was a popular attraction during the last quarter of the 20th century. A wooden board depicting a leaping horse and rider erected on the corner opposite White Hart House advertised the event to passers-by. The

Mothers' Union members' card 1957.

Oliver family of Clump House were the main organisers of the equestrian side, which was held in the morning. Many young riders from the area came to compete and swelled the attendance at the fete in the afternoon.

The Women's Institute, a popular village club, provided the refreshments for many of the village shows including the fete and gymkhana. The W.I. flourished in Chitterne between the wars and after, but gradually towards the end of last century the number of members dwindled so much that the club proved to be unviable and, despite the stalwart efforts of past president Kathleen Babey, it folded. The W.I. refreshment tent is no more, but the Annual Village Fete continues, now run in tandem with a well-attended dog show.

The last quarter of the village year brought the annual bonfire and fireworks, followed by Christmas celebrations. Tony and Marilyn Wood held some memora-

Chitterne Women's Institute meeting in the Village Hall. Left to right: Celia Watson; Sue Morgan; Lynne Cockburn; Kathleen Babey; Jean Nicholas; Anna Carter; Jeanne George.

ble bonfire parties in the sportsfield in the 1980s. Tony created unusual bonfires, which were eagerly anticipated by the village children. Today bonfire parties are still held, organised by the Cricket Club, who provide wonderful displays of fireworks.

In the past The King's Head has been the venue for performances by the mummers at Christmas. This would be one of a series of performances at selected public houses in the 20th century. But in the 19th century they performed at all the chief houses in the village.

It was quite clear that they only remembered fragments of what had once been a very much longer 'mummers' play. The portions they remembered did not seem to be consecutive and did not make any sense. They wore head-dresses made like mitres with coloured paper and tinsel, and their coats were adorned all over with ribbons of coloured paper or calico, and they were armed with wooden swords.[237]

By the end of the 20th century the play still made no sense but that is part of the charm of this old tradition.

From time to time national celebrations occur and these have always been enthusiastically celebrated in Chitterne. The

Tony Wood's bonfire house 1986.

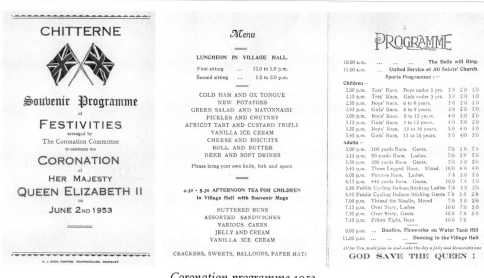

Coronation programme 1953.

coronation of George V in 1911 was marked by a crowded village banquet held in one of the village barns suitably decorated with bunting and union flags.

A village Coronation Committee arranged a programme of festivities to celebrate the coronation of Queen Elizabeth II on 2nd June 1953. In the morning the bells were rung and a service held in the church. Luncheon, provided in two sittings in the village hall, included cold ham and ox tongue with salad and new potatoes, followed by apricot tart or custard trifle and cheese and biscuits, washed down with beer and soft drinks. In the afternoon a series of races were organised for the children followed by afternoon tea in the hall of buns, sandwiches, cakes, jelly and cream and ice cream, with crackers, sweets, balloons and the presentation of coronation mugs. While the children were engaged in eating their tea the races for adults were held, including the pedal-cycling-balloon-sticking-race, needle threading race and a pillow fight for the boys. In the evening a bonfire and fireworks on Water Tank Hill, and dancing in the hall completed the celebrations.

The village hall was decorated with homemade bunting in red white and blue on the 29th July 1981 as the village celebrated the Royal Wedding of Prince Charles and Lady Diana Spencer. A fancy dress parade was one of the highlights. Little Victoria Morris who came as the Royal Wedding Cake won best fancy dress. Alternative races were held in the sportsfield, such as the beer and bandages race, and all the village children received commemorative mugs.

The Millennium celebrations held in the summer of 2000 had a similar format to coronation celebrations. The usual bell-ringing and church service, Shrewton

Silver Band on the sportsfield, sports, displays and entertainments were augmented by television in-fluenced items such as the Bronze Age warrior bust from Meet the Ancestors and a slide show and lecture on local archaeology. The army demonstrated a computer which analysed gun noise. In the evening a live band played in the Village Hall and

The old village hall decorated with home-made bunting for the 1981 Royal Wedding celebrations. Bert Bailey in the forground.

a hog was roasted and eaten and washed down with drinks from the licensed bar. In addition to these entertainments a photograph was taken from the top of the church tower of all those villagers present, and a time capsule encased in a mahogany box, made by village carpenter Nick Windsor, was due to be buried at St Mary's Chancel. This last event was postponed.

The village celebrated Queen Elizabeth's Golden Jubilee with a series of events on the 2nd and 3rd of June 2002. The bells were rung, a bonfire and fireworks lit, and a presentation made to the village children; jubilee coins this time. Rather than formal sit-down meals and races there were bring-your-own picnics on the sportsfield

and games. 21st century entertainment in-cluded Karaoke, coach trips on the Plain, dis-plays of memorabilia, competitions and a cricket match. The Golden Jubilee was per-manently commemorated by the erection of a smart new pair of Jubilee Gates at the side entrance to the churchyard. These were crafted in the village by Alan Sprack.

We have looked at the appearance and facilities of the new Village Hall in 'A Village Tour'. As with all old and loved buildings

Fred Babey handing out jubilee coins to Chitterne children in 2002.

some mourned the passing of the old school/ hall in 1998; the home perhaps of happy childhood memories. For others the opposite may have been true, and those people may have welcomed its demise. Now, eight years have passed since the opening of the new hall in 1999 and the building has settled into its space near The Green as if it has always been there. It is home to several

Alan and Maureen Sprack standing in front of Alan's jubilee gates 2002.

clubs: Sticky Fingers: the busy Parent and Toddler group, the Sunday Club for children, Yoga Essence to keep us fit, the village Coffee and Chat Club, the Cricket Club on match days; it hosts meetings of all sorts and operates as a polling station at elections, as a committee room for meetings, as an exhibition hall for displays of art, as a dining room for lunches, teas and dinners, as a sales area for bazaars and as a refreshment station at fetes and festivals, besides a host of private functions. A Village Hall Management Committee oversees the smooth running of the financial side while, with satisfying continuity, the caretaker and keyholder, Doris Windsor, is the same lady who used to keep the old school spick and span forty years ago.

For many years in the late 19th and 20th centuries Chitterne enjoyed a reputation for success in sport. 'The village has always produced some good sportsmen, and the recent generation are worthily maintaining the reputation the village has always had in this respect.'[238]

Both the village cricket and football teams achieved notable wins that led to this generally held opinion. But any successful village club depends on the willingness and steadfastness of the members. The fortunes of the village football club varied through the years, as did those of the cricket club and tennis club, with the constant waxing and waning of suitable talent and interest. At this point in time we have a successful Chitterne Cricket Club but no tennis or football club, however, in the past, Chitterne footballers were the best team in the Warminster area.

A meeting to discuss starting a football club in Chitterne was first held in 1902. By the early 1920s the Chitterne Football Club was thriving and by 1923 had reached its zenith, by winning the Warminster Hospital Cup for the third season running. The Chitterne team played as far afield as Mere where in 1931, in terrible conditions of rain and sleet, one of the team's longest serving players, Frank Bailey, went off in a state of collapse and Chitterne lost 2-0. However, in 1932 Frank was a member of the victorious Chitterne team that won the cup at a six-a-side tournament held at Lavington, beating the Lavington team by ten points to one in the final. The rest of the team were J. Feltham, A. Polden, P. Potter, E. Cruse and A. Collins.[239]

The victorious Chitterne Football Team three times winners of the Warminster Hospital Cup 1923. Back row left to right: Dick Bailey; Lewis Feltham; unknown; George Bailey; Ted Sheppard. Middle row: Ted Bailey; Fred Grant; Alban Polden; Frank Bailey; Harry Sheppard; Stan Feltham; unknown; Owen Polden; Bill Bartlett. Front row: Frank Grant; Stan Grant; Evelyn Feltham; unknown; unknown; Bill Spratt.

Such was the enthusiasm in the village for playing football that young talent was nurtured alongside the adult team. Young Chitterne footballers did well in the Wiltshire Junior Cup competition in 1932, keeping up the village tradition of producing good footballers.[240] The youth team later folded but interest was revived in

January 1957 with Leonard Knock, the postmaster from Bidden Lane, as coach. The Chitterne Boys Under-13 Football Team played their first game away against the Sutton Veny team of the same age and only just lost the match at 3 goals to 2.

King's Head Darts Team c.195? Back row left to right: Dick Bailey; Colin Gorry; David Phelps; Arthur Polden; Denis Blake. Front: Ray Poolman; Cecil Newton (landlord); Richard Feltham; John Patterson.

This game generated a lot of excitement amongst the younger generation. Afterwards the Chitterne Team Captain said they were looking forward to a return match with Sutton Veny and being challenged by any other similar teams in the area.[241] However, Chitterne lost the return match and eventually this youth team also folded. By the 1970s there was no youth or adult village team.

A tennis club thrived before World War II and less energetic sports and games such as darts; skittles; crib and dominoes were played in the public houses. Stout warmed with a red-hot poker from the fire and a pinch of ginger went down well amongst the players. Regulars were Alf Burt, Ev Feltham, Tom Gorry and Sid Pearce who occupied the settle. In the 1950s Cecil Newton hosted The King's Head Darts Team's regular matches. For a few years darts was replaced by pool as the pub game of choice, but now neither game is played.

We do not know when Chitterne Cricket Club was first created, but it enjoyed a lot of success in the early 1880s. Members of the team were rightly proud of their achievements despite the 'thoroughly bad' pitch, which they prepared as best they could. Sometimes they played four entertaining innings in five hours of a Saturday. Among their number, and their inspiration, was Robert Blake, a local farmer who played for the Wiltshire County team. He was 'a good steady bowler, one of the best fields in the slips, and a cheerful batsman who usually made over thirty runs in twenty minutes'. The vicar's sons, William and Edward Swayne, played. William was a medium fast bowler and Edward, the better cricketer of the two, was 'a pretty bat and sometimes a devastating bowler, especially with Robert Blake in the slips'. There were two of three other village lads who were 'cheerful batsmen' and the whole team was better than other village teams in the field. But that was not all, for the team had a secret weapon, a long lean man, solemn faced, aged about thirty years. He had a good eye, and he sometimes made runs, usually hitting the ball out of the field, but he excelled as a bowler. He was known only as 'Shepherd'.

'If our regular bowlers were held up, a murmur would arise from the fieldsmen as they crossed over, 'What about Shepherd. Try Shepherd'. Shepherd was accordingly put on. He wore hob-nailed boots and black trousers, a many-coloured shirt, and his sleeves were turned up almost to his shoulders, exhibiting a remarkably long, brown muscular arm. He was an old-fashioned under-hand bowler. Never have I seen under-hand bowled at a greater pace, or with a more utter disregard of pitch. Sometimes the ball did not pitch at all, but sped straight from Shepherd's muscular hand to the wicket. Sometimes it was body-line bowling with a vengeance. Sometimes the ball

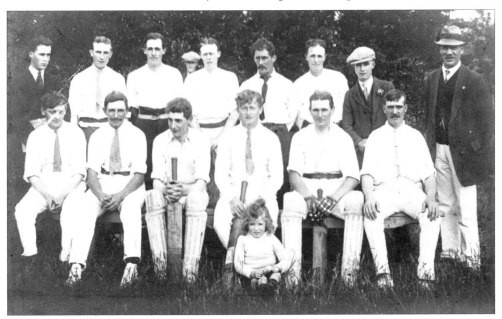

Chitterne Cricket Team 1921. Back row left to right: Ted Sheppard; George Bailey; Stan Feltham; Herbie Feltham; Fred (Bammer) Poolman; Archie Feltham; Frank Bailey; Bill Bartlett. Front: Walter Herrington; Fred Feltham; Johnny Webster; Stan Herrington with Willie Ashley between his feet; Lewis Feltham; Harry (Gunner) Poolman.

pitched less than half-way, and as the pitch was by no means too perfect, kicked and broke at any angle and in all directions. It was the kind of bowling which caused wrath on the part of some of our opponents who thought they knew how cricket ought to be played. It was bowling which needed to be carefully watched, and sometimes needed to be carefully left alone. The result was that in two or three overs Shepherd often secured a couple of wickets, caught more often than bowled. It was then time to put our regular bowlers on again, and Shepherd returned to his place in the field with extreme solemnity.[242]

Cricket Match on the sportsfield 2002.

Cricket matches were played at several venues around the village in days gone by, none of which were ideal. One such venue was the first big field on the left after the horse paddock on the Codford road; another was the field to the right of Elm Farm Path, above and behind the chalk pit. Despite the lack of a good pitch the Cricket Club thrived. Henry Slater and Lily Poolman hosted the Cricket Club's supper evening at the Bridge Café for many years in the 1940s and early 1950s when Arthur Spratt was the team Captain.[243] But the younger village cricketers drifted away and in about 1959 the club folded due to a lack of players.

The cricket club was re-formed in 2001, with a view to organising friendly local matches on Sundays in the sportsfield. By early 2002 there were 45 members aged 16 to 70. The club was awarded £1000 for a cricket net, and £666 for equipment by Awards For All (National Lottery), and £250 by West Wilts District Council. The club tendered for, and won, the contract to cut the sportsfield grass; they made great efforts to improve the whole sportsfield and especially the wicket, resulting in a pitch to be proud of at last. The clubs efforts expanded to include the general clearing of the area around The Cut. An enthusiastic tidying up ensued and led to Chitterne winning the small village section of the Best Kept Village Competition in 2004. Today the view presented to the visitor approaching the centre of the village from Shrewton is much improved, especially if a cricket match is in progress, thanks to the efforts of the Cricket Club. The most recent addition to the facilities is the new shed, which was erected in 2006. Home cricket matches are held every other Sunday and the team have won most of their matches under the captaincy of Charles Horsfall. The Chitterne cricket teas served in the village hall have gained a reputation for excellence; ensuring enthusiastic return visits from away players.

Chitterne Sportsfield from the St Mary's close end.

Glossary

Ansty Hill hill leading off the plain on Heytesbury road

Arch bridge over brook at Townsend near Abdon Close

Back Lane from Elm Farm to Pitt's Cottage

Back Path from the Dring to Back Lane

Back Road from Pitt's Cottage to Chitterne Farm

Baggerbush from Grump Path to junction of Tyning Path and Dirty Road

Benevolence a forced loan or contribution exacted by the King from his subjects

Bidden Lane the road heading to Shrewton from White Hart corner

Bourne the Chitterne Brook at the Tilshead end of the village

Breach Hill hill from Middle Barn towards Tilshead

Breakheart Bottom dry valley to north-west of village

Breakheart Hill hill up the Hollow

Carucate measure of land in middle England comparable to a hide

Chalk Pit pit in Back Lane where chalk was dug for building

Chitterne Ansty hamlet between Chitterne and Knook

Churches Path or **Top Road** path from opposite number 1 Townsend to St Marys' Church-yard

Clay Pits the hill between Codford and Shrewton roads where clay was dug in 17th C

Clump Farm Bridge old bridge over brook opposite Clump House

Cob method of wall-building using chalk, flints, chaff etc.

Compton's Bridge bridge over brook at Bridge Cottage

Copehill Down site of FIBUA village

Copyholder tenant who held land by copy of the court roll; a villein in medieval times

Cottager occupier, possibly owner, of a tenement with a small amount of land

Cut local name for the Chitterne Brook in the village

Dring lane off Bidden Lane between numbers 67 and 68, leading into Back Path

FIBUA village Fighting In Built Up Areas training village on Copehill Down

Flemming's Bargain former farm in Chitterne St Mary location unknown

Free Warren permission from the Crown to kill or keep game and beasts

Gallybagger Corner corner of the Heytesbury road by the Hollow, where scarecrows once stood

Gasson Garston, the field behind St Mary's Close and the sportsfield

Glebe land held by a clergyman

Glebe Terrier inventory of land held by a clergyman

Groat four pence

Grump Path from behind number 1 Townsend to numbers 20 and 22 Townsend

Hide between 60 and 100 acres of land, depending on quality

Hile Wiltshire word for a stook (of sheaves)

Hollow part of the old coach road to Warminster opposite The Round House

Housecarl a member of the King's personal guard

Hut former venue for village social gatherings in Bidden Lane

Imber Range live firing range to the west of Chitterne

Imber Range Perimeter Path public right of way around the Imber Range

Jubilee Gates alongside the church, erected 2002

Jubilee Tree horse chestnut tree on the Green, planted 1897

Kissing gate a gate in a U or V shaped enclosure allowing only one person through at a time

Kite Hill hill beyond Chitterne Dairy track to left of Codford road

Lane Bidden Lane or Shrewton Road

Lengthman person whose job was to maintain a particular length of road

Linches Path path in front of Chitterne Farm Cottages heading to Tilshead

London Road former coach road near Middle Barn

Long Hedge Path Mead track that passes Glebe Farm buildings to Spot's Pool

Long Trees line of trees along parish boundary towards Chitterne Ansty

Maddington former village now part of Shrewton

Padham's Pool winterbourne pool near Middle Barn

Penny Reading Room in Back Lane

Pitt's Lane from Pitt's Cottage to village road

Rowleaze former name of farm land, location not known

Southern Range Road exclusive army road passes north-west of Chitterne

Spot's Pool pool on right of Codford Road near parish boundary

Street Heytesbury Road from Bridge Cottage to the Round House

Tyning Path from the junction of Elm Farm track and Long Hill to Baggerbush

Villein an unfree tenant in medieval times

Virgate a quarter of a hide, depending on soil quality anything between 15 to 60 acres

Walk path on the bank of the Cut from Manor Farm to the sportsfield

Wether Castrated male sheep

Whitsuntide Field former name of sportsfield

Winterbourne a stream that runs dry in the summer months

Notes

1 Alan Moore, writer.
2 www.round-house.demon.co.uk/history
3 The Field Archaeology of the Salisbury Plain Training Area
4 The Teacher's Aid 1893/4.
5 Also spelt Syfrewast or Cyfrewast
6 See Praying and Learning
7 British History Online: british-history.ac.uk
8 1742/1433. WSRO.
9 Also spelt Temmse or Temmes
10 Jordan Papers: Katy Jordan.
11 Deed of ffeofment: Katy Jordan.
12 947/1436 WSRO.
13 Will of Benjamin Giles, 1709.
14 1742/1430 WSRO.
15 Rev. W.H. Jones: Bradford-on-Avon: a history and description, chapter 6.
16 Bowles. Chap.xv p.291-2.
17 See A Village Tour
18 Rev. J.T. Canner: History of Chitterne.
19 Research by Ken Michell.
20 See Farming.

21 947/1456 WSRO.
22 Wilts Glebe Terriers.
23 1742/1430 WSRO.
24 947/1459 Long. WSRO.
25 Interview of Misses Feltham by E. Nixon-Eckersall. 1975.
26 947/2091 1877 WSRO.
27 Round House deeds.
28 1896 Sale particulars. WSRO.
29 Memories: Walter H Long.
30 See Village People.
31 Canner: Notes on History of Chitterne.
32 Inquisitiones Nonarum 1341
33 A History of the County of Wiltshire. Vol 3: College of de Vaux, Salisbury.
34 Opinion of Judith Patrick, Architectural historian, 2004.
35 As told by Nora Feltham to Joan Robertson.
36 Statement signed by William Dyer, Incumbent of Imber and JH Johnson, vicar of Tilshead.
37 See A Village Tour.
38 Refers to the Baptists who met in Bidden Lane.
39 Ernie George: Writings.
40 Interview with Diana Sanders, 2006.
41 See A Village Tour.
42 Grant Family History: Roy Grant.
43 Maidment papers.
44 See Village People.
45 Baptist Church Minute Book 1883-1938.
46 See 'How to Make a Cob Wall' in Earning a Living.
47 1841 census.
48 1851 census.
49 1861 census.
50 Interview with William Brown in Teacher's Aid 1893/4.
51 Interview with Pam Jones (née Poolman) and Connie Gorry(née Grant), 2005.
52 Lee Hamilton, granddaughter of Elizabeth Stokes.
53 Interview with Beryl & Nora Feltham by Mrs Nixon-Ekersall 1975.
54 Warminster & Westbury Journal: 7 March, 1903.
55 See Village People.
56 Ernie George: Writings.
57 Ernie George: Writings.
58 See Farming.
59 Norman Bowler Reminiscences.
60 Warminster Journal: 17 Dec 1954.
61 Interview with Diana Sanders (née Dean), 2006.
62 For more detail try Ancient Trackways of Wessex, by HW Timperley and Edith Brill.
63 Edith Olivier Journals 1924-48.
64 'She mustn't be frightened at what she saw for they wouldn't hurt her'.
65 Canner's History of Chitterne.
66 John Daniel's History of Warminster.
67 Trustees elected 1783. WRSO
68 Turnpike accounts 1780. WRSO
69 Land tax document 1784. WRSO
70 Samuel Pepys' Diaries 1668-9.
71 Reminiscences of Percy Maidment, grandson of Frank, 2005.
72 Warminster & Westbury Journal. Mr Allsop lived at the Gate House.
73 Reminiscences of Laurie Wallis, 2000.
74 Survey by Diana Dean at Chitterne School, 1965, (no relation to the Imber Deans).
75 Survey by Diana Dean, Chitterne School 1965.
76 2001 census.
77 Survey by Diana Dean, Chitterne School 1965.
78 1881 census.
79 See Earning a Living.
80 See Earning a Living.
81 1881 census.
82 1881 census.
83 See Earning a Living.
84 Andrews and Drury Map 1773.
85 Listed buildings, Images of England.
86 'Down Wiltshire Way' tape 1994.
87 Canner's History of Chitterne.
88 Will of William Jordan, 1602: Katy Jordan.
89 Canner's History of Chitterne.
90 Hoare
91 Reminiscences of Mr Allsop.
92 Also spelt Temmse or Temmes.
93 Salisbury Journal & Devizes Gazette 22 April 1852.
94 947/1440 WSRO
95 See Fun and Games.
96 Ernie George family history.
97 Reminiscences of Graham & Linda Dean.
98 See Earning a Living.
99 See Fun and Games.
100 See Village People.
101 See Earning a Living.
102 1841 census.
103 See Tracks and Robbers.
104 Ernie George, old photographs. See Praying and Learning.
105 See Tracks and Robbers.
106 See Earning a Living.
107 Sale Brochure 1896.
108 Court Rolls.
109 See Farming.
110 Baptist Minute Book 1883 – 1938.
111 See Village People.

112 See Earning a Living.
113 Reminiscences of Graham and Linda Dean.
114 1742/1428 Methuen docs WSRO.

115 1896 Sale particulars.
116 See Earning a Living.
117 See Farming.
118 Reminiscences of Laurie Wallis.
119 Recollections of William E Sanders.
120 See Farming.
121 See www.round-house.demon.co.uk/history for more detail.
122 See Farming.
123 Kellys Directory, 1927.
124 See Farming.
125 George Macaulay Trevelyan.
126 Laurie Wallis, 2000.
127 Wallis Family Tree: Rupert Lionel Wallis, courtesy of Kay Findley.
128 Letters written by Alice and Louisa in possession of family of Max Newman, Texas, USA.
129 Compton Family Tree: Catherine Koppana.
130 Court Rolls.
131 See Farming and Praying and Learning.
132 Warminster Journal 16 January 1931.
133 Ashley Family Tree: Peter Ashley.
134 Grant Family Tree: Roy Grant.
135 Reminiscences of Connie Gorry née Grant.
136 Poolman Family Tree: Pat Ricketts.
137 See Earning a Living.
138 Bill Windsor, Abdon's great grandson.
139 History of Chitterne: Rev. JT Canner.
140 Warminster Journal: 14 April 1906.
141 History of Chitterne: Rev JT Canner.
142 The Illustrated Warminster and District Miscellany, Vol. 1.
143 Ernie George. See Fun and Games.
144 Ray Feltham.
145 1851 census.
146 Kelly's 1875.
147 Bertillonage-Black Museum.
148 Metropolitan Police Archives: Maggie Bird.
149 See Farming.
150 The Windmills of John Wallis Titt: J. Kenneth Major. 1977.
151 Maidment papers: Percy & Ivy Maidment.
152 T. Darvill, P. Stamper & J. Timby: England, an Archaeological Guide.
153 John T. Canner: The History of Chitterne. 1925.
154 British-history.ac.uk
155 Wiltshire Windmills: Martin Watts. 1980.
156 Will of William Jordan, 1602: Katy Jordan.
157 Olivia George: Essay 1887.

158 W. Laurence B. Wallis of The Manor, Chitterne. 2005.
159 Interview with Mr Brown from 'Teacher's Aid' 1893/4.
160 Interview with the Felthan Sisters by Mrs Nickerson-Ekersall. 1975.
161 Reminiscences of Victor Feltham.
162 Parson's Pleasure: W.S.Swayne 1934. Chapter 3.
163 Parson's Pleasure: W.S.Swayne 1934. Chapter 3.
164 Fred Babey, retired farmer, Chitterne Farm.
165 Fred Babey, retired farmer, Chitterne Farm.
166 Hoare: Modern History of Wiltshire. 1824.
167 Goddard from Salisbury Journal July 29 1905.
168 Wiltshire Windmills: Martin Watts. 1980.
169 British History Online: british-history.ac.uk
170 See 'Lords of the Manors' chapter.
171 See 'A Village Tour' chapter.
172 1851 census.
173 1881 census.
174 Kelly's Directory 1927.
175 Warminster Journal, 1 July 1983.
176 William Windsor, Chitterne. 2005.
177 John T. Canner: Church Visiting Book 1904-25.
178 Ernie George, reminiscences and sketch of New Barn 1933.
179 Bill Windsor.
180 Max Newman.
181 Court Rolls.
182 Kelly's Directory 1890.
183 Kelly's Directory 1927.
184 Daisy Sheppard.
185 Laurie Wallis.
186 Graham and Linda Dean.
187 Fred & Kathleen Babey: Farming in Chitterne 1955-2000.
188 Chris Corden: The Plain 1998.
189 Ernie George: Writings.
190 Reminiscence by Lee Hamilton, granddaughter of Elizabeth Stokes 2006.
191 See Praying and Learning chapter.
192 Reminiscences of Pam Jones and Connie Gorry 2005.
193 Hoare: Modern Wiltshire.
194 Phillipp Gauntlett and Jonathan Gauntlet of Chitterne 1637, Marriage Licence Bonds.
195 947/1456 WSRO.
196 Hoare quoting Fuller: History of Worthies of England 1662.
197 Marriage Licence Bonds.
198 Will of 1717: P2/P/774 WSRO.
199 1851 census.
200 Kelly's Directory 1890.

201 Kelly's Directory 1875.
202 1881, 1901 censuses.
203 Chris Corden: The Plain 1998.
204 Rev. Canner's Visiting Book 1904-1925.
205 Interview with Graham & Linda Dean 2006.
206 1851 census.
207 Ernie George, old photographs.
208 Ernie George: Reminiscences of his uncle Edwin re: Thomas George c1820-1900.
209 Bill Windsor.
210 Warminster & Westbury Journal 16 Sep 1927.
211 Horse Racing History Online: www.horseracinghistory.co.uk
212 Jeanne George Archive.
213 Reminiscencesof Michael Sheppard, grandson of Frank 2006. 1925 Canner, 1927, Kelly's.
214 1851 census.
215 See A Village Tour chapter.
216 Wessex Water: Chitterne Pumping Station.
217 History of Chitterne: Rev. J.T.Canner
218 Parson's Pleasure: W.S.Swayne 1934. Chapter 3.
219 Warminster Journal, 28 Nov.1930.
220 Parson's Pleasure: W.S.Swayne 1934. Chapter 3.
221 Reminiscences of Bill Windsor, one of the cadets.
222 Email from Dave Bamford.
223 Interview with Connie Gorry, 2005.
224 Reminiscences of Ray Poolman.
225 Reminiscences of Bill Windsor.
226 Warminster Journal, Nov.1951.
227 Conversation with staff at Hartcliffe Community Council's Park Farm, Bristol.
228 Chitterne Village Hall Appeal, 1997.
229 W.S. Swayne: Parson's Pleasure, 1934. Chapter 3.
230 Ernie George: Writings.
231 Warminster Journal, 30 November 1901.
232 Bill Windsor: Reminiscences.
233 Ernie George: Writings.
234 Bill Windsor: Reminiscences.
235 Interview with Diana Sanders (née Dean), 2006.
236 Interview with Diana Sanders (née Dean), 2006.
237 W.S.Swayne: Parson's Pleasure, 1934. Chapter 3.
238 Warminster Journal, 15 January 1932.
239 Warminster Journal, 1 April 1932.
240 Warminster Journal 15 January, 1932.
241 Warminster Journal, 25 January 1957.
242 W.S. Swayne: Parson's Pleasure, 1934. Chapter 3.
243 Warminster Journal.

Index

NOTE: Places and clubs in Chitterne are indexed under CHITTERNE PLACES, and CLUBS. Page references in **bold** type refer to illustrations.